Good Practice Guide: **Negotiating the Planning Maze**

RIBA Good Practice Guides

Other titles in this series:

Good Practice Guide: Negotiating the Planning Maze

THIRD EDITION

John Collins, Consultant, Past President of the RTPI
Philip Moren, Planning Consultant

RIBA Publishing

© John Collins and Philip Moren, 2009
Published by RIBA Publishing, 15 Bonhill Street, London EC2P 2EA

First edition published 2002 as *A Guide to Negotiating the Planning Maze*
Second edition published 2006 as *Good Practice Guide: Negotiating the Planning Maze*
Revised and updated third edition published 2009

ISBN 978 1 85946 346 8

Stock Code 69963

British Library Cataloguing-in-Publication Data
A catalogue record for this book is available from the British Library.

Publisher: Steven Cross
Commissioning Editor: James Thompson
Project Editor: Alasdair Deas
Designed by Ben Millbank
Typeset by Academic + Technical
Printed and bound by MPG Books, Cornwall

The information contained in this book is given for guidance purposes only and does not purport to be a definitive statement of planning law, policy or practice. While every effort has been made to check its accuracy, neither the authors not the publishers can accept any responsibility for any actions based on the use of this guide, and they will not be liable for any consequent damages. Readers should therefore make their own checks. The views expressed are solely the opinions of the authors and do not reflect those of any client or employer.

RIBA Publishing is part of RIBA Enterprises Ltd.
www.ribaenterprises.com

Series foreword

The *Good Practice Guide* series has been developed specifically to provide architects, and other construction professionals, with practical advice and guidance on a range of topics that affect them, and the management of their business, on a day-to-day basis.

All the guides in the series are written in an easy-to-read, straightforward style. They are not meant to be definitive texts on the particular subject in question, but each guide will be the reader's first point of reference, offering them a quick overview of the key points and then providing them with a 'route map' for finding further, more detailed information. Where appropriate, checklists, tables, diagrams and case studies are included to aid ease of use.

Good Practice Guide: Negotiating the Planning Maze

Planning is an intrinsic and fundamental part of the way we shape the built environment, and all architects must become involved in planning to a greater or lesser extent. Yet for an architectural practice of any size, the planning process can often appear daunting in its bureaucracy and ever-changing complexity.

While the planning system continues to evolve, this deservedly popular guide – now in its third edition – has evolved with it. With admirable clarity and concision, it explains how the system works, outlines the ongoing reforms and guides the reader through the process of submitting a planning application. It also shows how you can get involved in plan-making and development management and very clearly outlines what to do when things go wrong.

The key message is that architects (and, indeed, *all* construction professionals) need to work together with planners in order for the best results to be achieved. This thorough and extensive book should be required reading for all architects, as it promotes exactly this kind of understanding.

Ruth Reed
President, RIBA

Preface

We write this preface during the bicentenary year of the birth of Charles Darwin, father of evolution, with over three years having now passed since the last edition of this guide was published. At that time, we were anticipating the much-heralded new era in planning to be brought about by the reforms of the Planning and Compulsory Purchase Act 2004, which had just received its Royal Assent. Like mankind, the planning system was not created perfect, but has evolved over time. And so it is that the system continues to develop and adapt – at times painfully slowly, most would agree – to changing circumstances and new challenges.

The 2004 Act has been introduced in stages, and has been supplemented by secondary legislation and additional government guidance. These new provisions have altered the shape and complexity of the *planning maze* significantly. To many struggling to find their way around the maze, however, the unintended effect of the reforms was to make it even trickier to negotiate. Practitioners have had to adapt to these changes. We have all had to learn new tricks and tactics, and become familiar with an ever-expanding set of planning terms and requirements.

The government's desire for reform, bolstered by private sector interest groups who see planning as an obstacle to economic growth, has not stopped with the 2004 Act. Soon after it was passed, another planning reform bill was on its way – on the heels of a planning White Paper published in 2007 that had carried forward recommendations by Kate Barker in her review of land use planning, together with those by Rod Eddington in his review on the reform of major transport infrastructure planning. The resulting Planning Act 2008 provided for the establishment of an Infrastructure Planning Commission to deal with nationally significant infrastructure projects, as well as setting out further changes to the planning system and introducing a new kind of roof tax in the form of a Community Infrastructure Levy.

One might be forgiven for thinking that that would be the end of it for the time being. However, in the words of the Irish comedian Jimmy Cricket: 'there's more'. The government's thirst for planning reform is clearly unquenched. Not content with the Barker and Eddington Reviews, in March 2008 the government announced another new 'red tape busting review to weed out bureaucratic hurdles and create a more efficient planning service for the public and business'. This time, the Killian Pretty Review, whose final report was published in November 2008, concentrates on improving the planning application process from start to finish, to make it faster and more responsive. Its aim is to cut down on unnecessary paperwork and delays, including those after permission has been granted. The government's response in March 2009, which was followed by a further package of measures unveiled in July 2009, signals yet more changes in the months and years to come. Many of these, such as stream-lining information requirements for planning applications, are apparently intended to undo or relax some of the very changes only recently introduced!

Although the new plan-making regime is in full swing, this got off to a bad start in England when the first Development Plan Documents submitted to the Secretary of State for independent examination were rejected as 'unsound'. Many planning authorities responded to this setback by withdrawing their own emerging plans or delaying work on their preparation. So, some three years after the new system had started, instead of the government's target of 80 per cent of all local authorities having adopted a new-style Core Strategy being met, the figure was closer to 8 per cent. The new process was criticised for being overcompli-cated and repetitive, resulting in consultation fatigue and delays. During 2008, it was therefore revised again. Amended regulations and guidance have cut down the number of formal plan-making stages and are less prescriptive. Plan-ning authorities now have greater freedom to decide which plans they want to prepare and when, and how to involve the community in their preparation.

Meanwhile, extended transitional arrangements are in place. Many of the policies from old-style development plans have been saved under directions issued by the Secretary of State. And a very few plans are still being completed under the old provisions. Many areas are therefore covered by a patchwork quilt of adopted and emerging development plan policies. To add to this confusion, on 1 April 2009 the biggest restructuring in local government in England since 1974 saw 44 districts and counties replaced by nine 'supersized' unitary authorities.

The constant upheaval in the planning process places considerable demands on those who come up against it, in whatever role. The devastating effects of the current recession on the development industry have seen numerous projects mothballed or abandoned. It is therefore even more important that architects and other practitioners understand how the planning system works, in order to get positive results more quickly and at minimal cost to their clients, or simply to recognise those actions or proposed developments that are unlikely to succeed or be commercially viable.

Our updated guide outlines the recent and continuing reforms. It explains how you can get involved in plan-making and policy formulation, how best to approach the submission of planning applications and what to do when things go wrong. Above all, we hope that in these difficult times it will help you save time and money when seeking to add *intelligent design* to the evolving planning system.

John Collins and Philip Moren
November 2009

About the authors

John Collins OBE DipArch(Birm) SPDip RIBA FRTPI is a Past President of the Royal Town Planning Institute (RTPI) and a Past Regional Chairman of the RIBA in the Northwest, and has practised at different stages of his career as an architect and as a town planner. He has worked in local government in Birmingham, Coventry and latterly as County Planner of Cheshire. This followed a four-year spell in the private sector as an associate in an architectural and planning consultancy. He has experienced life as a civil servant both in the UK and overseas and has run his own planning consultancy, including a short period on the board of a Development Corporation. Currently he is a consultant to the Tweed Nuttall Warburton practice in Chester and represents the RTPI and Urban Design Group on the city's Conservation Area Advisory Committee.

Philip Moren BA(Hons) MRTPI is a planning consultant and writes extensively on planning issues. He has worked for three local authorities and two national consultancies. His current responsibilities include acting as a consultant Inspector with An Bord Pleanála, dealing with planning appeals in the Republic of Ireland. He is also a regular contributor to *Development Control Practice*, one of the planning profession's main reference works. For several years, he was co-compiler of *Planning* magazine's *Development Control Casebook* – a weekly legal and planning appeals digest – and editor of its *Forum* Q&A slot, in which he replied to readers' planning queries. He has extensive experience of the planning systems in England, Wales, Ireland and the Isle of Man, advising both public and private sector clients, and has been a guest speaker at various seminars and workshops for property professionals, including RIBA and RTPI CPD events.

Acknowledgements

We would like to thank all those people who made their individual contributions to the preparation of this guide in all its guises, especially:

Edward Barnes, Walker, Smith & Way; James Brotherhood, James Brotherhood Associates; Christopher Brummitt, Christopher Brummitt Architects; Anthony Burgess, Planning Portal; Dave Chetwyn, Stoke-on-Trent City Council; Murray Graham, Susan Hughes & Associates; Nick Taylor, Wigan MBC; Daniel Thompson, CABE; John Tweed, Tweed Nuttall Warburton; Tony H. Walton, retired architect and town planner; Michael Wildblood, Wildblood Macdonald; and Chris Winter, Director, English Historic Towns Forum.

In addition, of course, Mary Webster who helped us with drawing up our flowcharts.

Last, but not least, Matthew Thompson, James Thompson, Alasdair Deas and the editorial team at RIBA Publishing.

Contents

List of planning abbreviations

AAP	Area Action Plan
AMR	Annual Monitoring Report
AONB	Area of Outstanding Natural Beauty
AQMA	Air quality management area
BRE	Building Research Establishment
CABE	Commission for Architecture and the Built Environment
CADW	Welsh Historic Monuments body
CCW	Countryside Council for Wales
CIL	Community Infrastructure Levy
CIS	Community Involvement Scheme (Welsh equivalent of SCI)
CLEUD	Certificate of lawfulness of existing use or development
CLG	Communities and Local Government – the government department that replaced ODPM in May 2006, with overall responsibility for planning
CLOPUD	Certificate of lawfulness of proposed use or development
DAS	Design and Access Statement
Defra	Department for Environment, Food and Rural Affairs
DETR	Department of the Environment, Transport and the Regions (responsible for planning prior to 2001)
DfT	Department for Transport
DoE	Department of the Environment (predecessor to DETR)
DPD	Development Plan Document
DTLR	Department of Transport, Local Government and the Regions (responsible for planning between 2001 and 2002)
EIA	Environmental Impact Assessment
EiP	Examination in Public (into a draft revised RSS)
ES	Environmental Statement

ESDP	The European Spatial Development Perspective
FRA	Flood risk assessment
GDPO	The Town and Country Planning (General Development Procedure) Order 1995
GPDO	The Town and Country Planning (General Permitted Development) Order 1995
HAC	Heritage asset consent
HAS	Householder Appeals Service (PINS)
IPC	Infrastructure Planning Commission
LDC	Lawful development certificate (certificate of lawfulness)
LDD	Local Development Document
LDF	Local Development Framework
LDO	Local Development Order
LDP	Local Development Plan (new-style development plan in Wales)
LDS	Local Development Scheme
LPA	Local planning authority, i.e. unitary authorities and district councils, but used in this guide to include county councils where relevant to their role in producing minerals and waste LDDs
LTP	Local Transport Plan
MIPPS	Ministerial Interim Planning Policy Statement (for Wales)
NAW	National Assembly for Wales
ODPM	Office of the Deputy Prime Minister, responsible for planning between May 2002 and 6 May 2006 (superseded by CLG)
OS	Ordnance Survey
PD	Permitted Development rights under the GPDO
PINS	The Planning Inspectorate
PPG	Planning Policy Guidance note
PPS	Planning Policy Statement, previously PPG
PPW	Planning Policy Wales
RPG	Regional Planning Guidance
RPB	Regional planning body
RSS	Regional Spatial Strategy, taken in this guide to include the Spatial Development Strategy (SDS) in London
RTPI	Royal Town Planning Institute
RTS	Regional Transport Strategy
SA	Sustainability Appraisal
SCI	Statement of Community Involvement

SCS	Sustainable Community Strategy
SEA	Strategic Environmental Assessment
SHLAA	Strategic Housing Land Availability Assessment
SI	Statutory instrument
SoS	Secretary of State with overall responsibility for planning matters, currently in England the Secretary of State for Communities and Local Government (in Wales, the National Assembly under the First Minister)
SPD	Supplementary Planning Document
SPG	Supplementary Planning Guidance
SPZ	Simplified Planning Zone
SSSI	Site of Special Scientific Interest
TAN	Technical Advice Note
TPO	Tree Preservation Order
UDP	Old-style Unitary Development Plan
VDS	Village Design Statement
WAG	Welsh Assembly Government
WO	Welsh Office

Introduction
Working together

In this Section:

- *What guidance are you looking for?*
- *Tips on using this guide*
- *Reform and evolution of the planning system since 2004*
- *Spatial planning and sustainable development*

Town planners and architects are not always the cosiest of bedfellows. To quote from a *RIBA Journal* report on the RIBAnet discussion forum: 'members return to a favourite subject: are planners dim, incompetent or just spineless?' Some planners are heard to ask similarly unflattering questions about architects.

The main job of this guide is to help members of the built environment professions to work together as one team. This can only be achieved when each has confidence and trust in the other's abilities, and a clear understanding of everyone's responsibilities. This guide aims to develop that understanding.

In a foreword to the *Citizen's Guide to Town and Country Planning*, first published by the Town and Country Planning Association in 1986, the late Anthony Greenwood, then Minister of Housing and Local Government, wrote:

> Plans to reshape towns or to preserve the countryside, and the countless decisions on individual planning applications, are too often inadequately explained. Prejudice and misunderstanding come from lack of clear information.

It is not only citizens, but also the many architectural practitioners and others caught up in the planning process – *the planning maze* – who find themselves in need of clear information and guidance. We hope that this guide will help you find your way through the maze.

1

What guidance are you looking for?

An exhaustive library of information has been published and is available, not least on the internet, covering all aspects of the complex system of town and country planning in the UK. This guide aims to provide a distillation of material of most use to architects, in a concise form. That does mean, of course, that we have had to leave much out. We have not, for example, included anything on the very complicated compulsory purchase and compensation regime, which, like the planning system itself, has been overhauled. However, any deficiencies should be remedied by following the links to the main sources of further information included at Appendix A.

This guide provides an outline of the framework of plan-making and development control in England and Wales, and seeks to address practitioners' primary concerns:

- How can I avoid common pitfalls?
- What are the most effective methods of dealing successfully with the planning bureaucracy?
- Where can I get more information and keep abreast of the complex and ever-changing planning law and practice?

Tips on using this guide

This guide deals mainly with planning in England, although we have tried to highlight the differences with the similar system in Wales, where appropriate. Because Wales is increasingly doing things its own way, and has not implemented all the major reforms that have taken place in England, care must be taken when working within the Principality. While Northern Ireland, Scotland, the Channel Islands and the Isle of Man all operate their own variations of the same theme, these are based on different legislation and are thus beyond the scope of this guide. However, the planning essentials, as well as ways of dealing positively with the bureaucracy, are fairly universal.

While this guide is not intended to be a primary reference point on planning law, inevitably we have had to include much background material of a somewhat dry and rather legalistic nature. As far as practicable, we have tried to simplify this and have explained any unusual terms and expressions when they first appear. However, a useful glossary of basic planning terms may be found on the Planning Portal website (see Appendix A).

At the end of each section we have summarised very briefly the key points you should remember.

Reform and evolution of the planning system since 2004

The Planning and Compulsory Purchase Act 2004 ('the 2004 Act') brought about the biggest shake-up to the system in England and Wales since the Second World War.

In England, the Act gave statutory force to many of the significant reforms proposed by the government in its Green Paper *Planning: Delivering a fundamental change* (DTLR, 2001), whose stated aim was to make the planning and compulsory purchase systems 'faster, fairer and more predictable'. The publication of the Green Paper in December 2001 was followed by a frenzy of consultation papers, new regulations and replacement policy guidance dealing with a wide variety of topics.

The 2004 Act sought to streamline plan-making by scrapping county Structure Plans, seen by many as overlapping and contradictory, leaving a two-tier system of complementary Regional Spatial Strategies (RSSs) and Local Development Frameworks (LDFs). So, at regional level, statutory RSSs are being drawn up by regional planning bodies (whose powers are soon to be transferred to regional development agencies) to gradually replace Regional Planning Guidance (RPG). And, at district level, old-style Local and Unitary Development Plans are in the process of being replaced by LDFs. These comprise a portfolio of Local Development Documents (LDDs) that local planning authorities (LPAs) are obliged to prepare in line with a Local Development Scheme (LDS), and which include Development Plan Documents (DPDs). The key plan in all this is the Core Strategy, since this sets out the spatial vision for a local area. The 2004 Act made it a statutory requirement for both LDDs and RSSs to contribute to sustainable development, while the Planning Act 2008 has added a duty on LPAs to take action on climate change in their development plans. Of course, these obligations need to be balanced against the government's policy objectives for the planning system as a facilitator for economic growth and recovery.

The new plan-making provisions came into force on 28 September 2004. However, following difficulties and delays in getting Core Strategies adopted, procedures were revised again in 2008. In order to ensure a smooth changeover from the old development plan-making system to the new regime, the 2004 Act included transitional arrangements, some of which are still in place. The effect of these is that certain policies from old-style development plans have been saved and continue to have statutory force until replaced by new DPDs.

In Wales, Part 6 of the 2004 Act provided for a reformed development plan system as well as the statutory basis for a Wales Spatial Plan. This followed the consultation paper *Planning: Delivering for Wales*, published in January 2002, and subsequent ministerial statements. The new provisions came into force in October 2005. Under the new plan-making regime, the current single-tier plans are retained but will now be known as Local Development Plans (LDPs). These are intended to be simpler and more concise documents than the present UDPs. However, until such time as it is supplanted by a new-style LDP, transitional arrangements ensure that whatever constitutes the development plan for an area (be it a UDP, Structure Plan or Local Plan) will retain development plan status. There are also provisions for completing – under expedited procedures – certain emerging UDPs.

We explain the recently revised plan-making regime in Section 2.

Various changes have also been made in an attempt to make the processing of planning applications quicker and more efficient, although the sheer amount of paperwork required in order to get an application validated has risen dramatically. These changes are explained in Section 5. Frustratingly, the 2004 Act is being brought into force in stages. While its main provisions have already taken effect (following a staggering ten separate commencement orders), others are still outstanding and dependent on new or amended secondary legislation.

The Planning Act 2008 provided for the establishment of a new Infrastructure Planning Commission (IPC) to deal with nationally significant infrastructure projects, such as airports and power stations. It also sets out further reforms to the planning system, introduces a Community Infrastructure Levy (CIL), places a duty on LPAs to have regard to the desirability of achieving good design and makes certain changes to the appeals process.

In addition, the final report of the Killian Pretty Review of the planning application system in England, published in November 2008, contains no fewer than 17 recommendations to the government on ways of making the system even faster and more responsive. The government's response in March 2009, and subsequent progress report and package of reforms published in July 2009, confirmed that we can expect yet more changes. So you must be alert to these.

Spatial planning and sustainable development

As well as tackling climate change, the transformed planning system places emphasis on two key features: 'spatial planning' and 'sustainable development'. It is therefore essential you understand what these expressions mean.

Definitions of *spatial planning* are quite hard to find and vary. According to the RTPI's *New Vision for Planning* (2007), spatial planning involves 'critical thinking about space and places as the basis for action or intervention'. The government's Planning Policy Statement (PPS) 1, which sets out the overarching principles for the planning system, states that spatial planning 'goes beyond traditional land-use planning to bring together and integrate policies for the development and use of land with other policies and programmes that influence the nature of places and how they function'. However, as acknowledged in a 2007 research report prepared for the government, RTPI and others (*Shaping and Delivering Tomorrow's Places: Effective practice in spatial planning*, by UCL and Deloitte), there is little common understanding among key participants in the system as to what this all means in practice. The report therefore explains that the planning system is now more than ever concerned with acting as a co-ordinator, integrator and mediator of the spatial dimensions of wider policy streams. The focus is thus on addressing the factors that influence the nature and functioning of the places we live in and what is referred to as their 'liveability'.

The 2004 Act requires planning authorities to undertake their functions with a view to contributing to the achievement of *sustainable development*. The definition given by the World Commission on Environment and Development is one that is widely used: 'development that meets the needs of the present without compromising the ability of future generations to meet their own needs'. Not only are the principles of sustainable development fundamental to assessments of the merits of proposed developments when considered at the planning application stage, but also the new plan-making regime has introduced requirements for emerging development plans to be appraised to ensure that they are as environmentally sound and sustainable as possible. Such Sustain-ability Appraisals (SAs) apply to LDFs and RSSs alike. These development plans (and a range of other plans and programmes, including Local Transport Plans (LTPs), waste and minerals plans) are also subject to Strategic Environmental Assessment (SEA) under European Directive 2001/42/EC.

The government's commitment to sustainable development is set out in *Securing the Future: The UK Government Sustainable Development Strategy* in conjunction with *One Future – Different Paths: The UK's shared framework for sustainable development* (both published in March 2005). For further information on sustainable development, visit the Sustainable Development Commission's website at www.sd-commission.org.uk

Details of the government's approach can also be found at www.defra.gov.uk/sustainable/government

SUMMARY

- Town planners and architects must understand each other and work together.
- This guide aims to provide a distillation of material of most use to architects, and outlines the framework of plan-making and development management in England and Wales. However, the guide will also be of use to others struggling to find their way around the planning maze.
- The planning system has recently undergone its biggest shake-up since the Second World War. In England, the old plan-making regime has been scrapped to leave a two-tier system of Regional Spatial Strategies and Local Development Frameworks, and in Wales a simplified single-tier system of Local Development Plans. Some transitional arrangements are still in place.
- The transformed system is underpinned by the concepts of spatial planning and sustainable development.
- English local planning authorities must also take action on climate change in their development plans.
- Further changes to the planning application process are expected – you will need to be alert to the ongoing changes.

Section 1
Planning framework: an overview

In this Section:

- *Place shaping*
- *Legislation*
- *Government policies and advice*
- *Administration of the system*
- *How the development management/control system works*

Place shaping

In its Planning Policy Statements (PPSs), the UK government summarises the role of the planning system thus:

> Planning shapes the places where people live and work and the country we live in. It plays a key role in supporting the Government's wider social, environmental and economic objectives and for sustainable communities.

The creation of 'sustainable communities' thus lies at the heart of the planning system. The government defines these as:

> Places where people want to live and work, now and in the future. They meet the diverse needs of existing and future residents, are sensitive to their environment, and contribute to a high quality of life. They are safe and inclusive, well planned, built and run, and offer equality of opportunity and good services for all.

Planning is the statutory mechanism by which the development of land is managed in the public interest. It does this mainly through the preparation by local planning authorities (LPAs) of a *development plan* (which is explained below), and the consideration by them of planning applications against the policies and proposals in that plan, exercising their *development management*

> See also: Meaning of 'development plan', page 13

(previously called *development control*) function. Together with *enforcement*, these plan-making and development management functions form what some have described as the 'planning trinity'.

However, it is the development management function with which architects are most likely to have to work. Development management is the new term for dealing with development proposals under a spatial planning system. As the government's Planning Advisory Service puts it, development management involves translating the council's strategies into development and facilitating the delivery of proposals that will help shape the community. So it is not just a new name for development control, although this remains part of the suite of development management functions. Such control activities include the handling of planning applications, where 'material considerations' are assessed and weighed in the balance. Here, the planner is piggy-in-the-middle, having to reconcile the needs and aspirations of competing interests – in order to maintain an appropriate balance between the development industry, on the one hand, and the wider community on the other. This requires considering the long-term social, environmental, economic and resource impacts of development proposals, bearing in mind also the need to achieve sustainable patterns of land use and development.

Legislation

The current system is based mainly on the following primary legislation:

- Planning Act 2008
- Planning and Energy Act 2008
- Planning and Compulsory Purchase Act 2004
- Planning and Compensation Act 1991
- Town and Country Planning Act 1990
- Planning (Listed Buildings and Conservation Areas) Act 1990
- Planning (Hazardous Substances) Act 1990
- Planning (Consequential Provisions) Act 1990.

These acts are supplemented by a range of subordinate legislation in the form of statutory instruments, including a variety of development orders and rules and regulations, which deal with matters of detail.

Government policies and advice

The requirements of the planning legislation, the way in which the system should work in practice, and national planning policies are outlined in Planning (and Minerals) Policy Statements and Guidance Notes, Technical Advice Notes (for Wales only), circulars and in other government pronouncements. We say more about national planning policies and guidance in Section 2 (see also the list at Appendix A).

Administration of the system

The planning system is administered by LPAs. These include:

- regional planning bodies (including the Mayor of London) whose role, outside London, will be taken over shortly by unelected regional development agencies
- county councils (with transport, minerals and waste planning responsibilities)
- district councils
- unitary authorities (single-tier councils combining the functions of both county and district councils)
- National Park authorities
- other special bodies or arrangements set up to deal with certain planning functions in major regeneration or expansion areas, such as new-style urban development corporations/authorities such as the Olympic Delivery Authority, London Thames Gateway and the Milton Keynes Partnership.

In addition, the Secretary of State with overall responsibility for planning matters (currently the Secretary of State for Communities and Local Government), via a number of regional government offices, the National Assembly for Wales (through the First Secretary) and the Planning Inspectorate all play key roles in formulating policy, making development plans and determining applications for planning permission or similar consent.

Although town, parish and community councils must be consulted on, or notified of, certain applications, they have no decision-making powers. Their role in the planning process is therefore purely advisory.

The Planning Act 2008 provided for the setting up of an Infrastructure Planning Commission (IPC), an independent, single-purpose body to deal with nationally significant infrastructure projects at a national level. Such projects include major airport and port projects, improvements to the strategic road network, major new power generating facilities and facilities critical to energy security, and major reservoir and wastewater plant works. Under the new arrangements, decisions on applications for 'development consent' will be made within the framework of national policy statements on key infrastructure sectors, such as air transport and renewable energy, and these will be produced by ministers. The IPC will be accepting applications from the energy and transport sectors from 1 March 2010, with applications from other sectors being accepted in subsequent years. Since the number of such projects is likely to be very small (probably no more than around 25 each year), we do not say any more about the IPC in this guide. However, for further information see the IPC's website at http://infrastructure.independent.gov.uk

How the development management/control system works

The overarching objectives for the planning system in England are explained in *Planning Policy Statement 1: Delivering Sustainable Development* (PPS1), issued by the government in 2005. This is supplemented by a companion guide – *The Planning System: General principles* (ODPM, 2004). These documents make it clear that the government is committed to a *plan-led* system of development control (now management), underpinned by the overall aim of delivering sustainable development. Added to this is the new requirement for spatial planning to contribute to reducing emissions and stabilising climate change, and to take into account the unavoidable consequences of new development.

"The government is committed to a plan-led system of development control"

Section 38(6) of the Planning and Compulsory Purchase Act 2004 ('the 2004 Act') gives statutory force to the primacy of the development plan and, in effect, requires that decisions should be made in accordance with the development plan, unless material considerations indicate otherwise. Thus, applications that go against relevant policies in the plan should not be allowed unless there are good planning reasons to justify permission.

In Wales, broadly similar advice is set out in *Planning Policy Wales* (PPW) (NAW, March 2002), as amended by various Ministerial Interim Planning Policy Statements (MIPPSs).

Tests for decision-makers

Generally, the test for decision-makers is whether any proposed development would cause 'material harm', or 'unacceptable' harm to interests of acknowledged importance. However, in the case of conservation areas (as explained in Section 3), with listed buildings and in certain sensitive areas, a stricter test should be applied. Here it is necessary to avoid any harm, as opposed to just 'material harm'. The distinctions may appear subtle but are crucial and are not always understood, even by those responsible for operating the system.

See also:
Conservation
areas, page 36

Meaning of 'development plan'

Under the current plan-making regime, the development plan comprises the Regional Spatial Strategy (RSS) (or, in London, the Spatial Development Strategy) and the portfolio of Development Plan Documents (DPDs) prepared by district councils, unitary authorities, the Broads authority, National Park authorities and, in the case of minerals and waste, DPDs produced by county councils. Transitional arrangements are still in place, which mean that until they are replaced by a new DPD, certain policies in old-style development plans may have been saved under direction of the Secretary of State. Therefore, to check which documents make up any development plan, you should consult the relevant LPA's Local Development Scheme on its website, which will also include a list of any saved policies. In Wales, the development plan consists of the Local Development Plan (LDP) or, until its preparation, any saved old-style Unitary Development Plans (UDPs), Structure Plans and Local Plans.

For the purposes of section 38(6) of the 2004 Act, plans and policies must have been statutorily adopted (that is, finally approved) by the relevant authorities. However, emerging policies may be taken into account as material considerations, with the weight to be attached to them increasing as they progress through the plan-preparation process.

The documents that make up the development plan are summarised in Figure 1.1.

FIGURE 1.1: *Documents comprising the 'development plan'*

England	Wales
New regime	
Two-tier system: • Regional Spatial Strategy (including the London Spatial Development Strategy); plus • Development Plan Documents (DPDs): – core strategy – site-specific allocations DPD – area action plans – other DPDs – proposals map	Single-tier system: • Local Development Plan
Transitional period	
Any saved policies in old-style: • Structure Plans • Unitary Development Plans • Local Plan	

Material considerations

In principle, any consideration that relates to the use and development of land is capable of being a planning consideration, and over the years the scope of such considerations has widened. The courts have ruled that material considerations include the following (the list is not exhaustive):

• the development plan
• basic factors involved in land-use planning, such as the number, size, height, layout, siting, design and external appearance of buildings and the proposed means of access, together with landscaping, impact on the character and appearance of the area, existing and proposed living conditions, highway safety, ecology, archaeology, the availability of infrastructure, and other environmental considerations
• government statements of planning policy
• emerging policies in the form of draft departmental circulars and policy guidance, depending on the context

- the views of third parties
- planning gain and developer contributions (see Section 5, *Planning obligations, developer contributions and 'planning gain'*, page 107)
- availability of alternative sites
- public concerns about safety and perception of harm
- need, and national and local economic considerations
- 'enabling development' (viz. development that would achieve a significant benefit to a heritage asset but which would otherwise be rejected as being contrary to planning policy – refer to the English Heritage website for further information)
- the ability of LPAs to impose conditions
- precedent (for example, if a rear extension to a dwelling in a row of such dwellings is permitted, it may be inevitable that others will follow)
- personal hardship (in certain circumstances)
- sustainability
- issues of viability, and other financial considerations (in certain circumstances)
- certain social and cultural matters (for example, maintenance of the Welsh language and identity)
- existing site uses and characteristics, its planning history and the effect of not granting permission.

Considerations that are not material

Matters that are not material planning considerations include those regulated by other legislation; objections on moral grounds (for example, to betting, alcohol or sex-related uses); the effect of a proposed development on property values; the maintenance of private views of some cherished object or landscape (unless these coincide with important public views); and the protection of other individual interests, except where these are also in the interests of the public as a whole. Legal restrictions, such as covenants, easements and rights of way, or commercial competition (in itself) are thus not relevant when considering a planning application.

Balancing considerations

The companion guide to PPS1 explains that if the development plan contains relevant policies, and there are *no* other material considerations, the application (or appeal) should be decided in accordance with the development plan. However, where there are other material considerations, the development plan should be the starting point, and the other material considerations weighed in the balance when reaching a decision. One such consideration will be whether the plan policies are relevant and up to date. They might, for example, have been overtaken by events or superseded by more recent government planning policy guidance. The 2004 Act provides that if there is a conflict between policies in an RSS and in a DPD, the most recent policy takes precedence.

Where an LPA proposes to grant planning permission for a development that is a significant departure from the development plan, the Secretary of State must be notified. The Secretary of State will then consider whether to intervene by 'calling in' and deciding the application, following a report by a government planning inspector.

Making proposed developments acceptable

When dealing with an application for planning permission or other consent, a planning authority may request amendments or improvements to the submitted proposal, impose conditions on the permission or consent, or require the applicant to enter into a 'planning obligation' in respect of the use or development of the application site or of other land or buildings. These matters are explained in Section 5.

See also:
Planning obligations, developer contributions and 'planning gain', page 107

SUMMARY

- 'Sustainable communities' are the heart of the planning system.
- The 'development plan' is the principal element in development management – in England, this consists of a Regional Spatial Strategy and a portfolio of Development Plan Documents, the nature and content of which will vary according to the needs of specific areas. In Wales, the new plan-making regime provides for a single-tier Local Development Plan. However, under extended transitional arrangements in both nations the development plan may include certain saved policies from old-style development plans.
- Development plans are prepared by local planning authorities in accordance with government policies and guidelines.
- The planning system is required to consider a wide range of factors when assessing applications for permission, with the development plan being the primary consideration. However, development management must operate in the interests of the public as a whole.

Section 2
The hierarchy of planning policy and development plans

In this Section:

- *The European Spatial Development Perspective*
- *National planning policy and guidance*
- *Regional Spatial Strategies and Regional Planning Guidance*
- *Structure Plans*
- *Local Development Frameworks, Local Plans and Supplementary Planning Documents*
- *Minerals and waste local plans*
- *Unitary Development Plans*
- *The Spatial Development Strategy for London*

Figure 2.1 (page 20) summarises the hierarchy of planning policy and development plans that apply to England and Wales, as explained in this Section.

The European Spatial Development Perspective

Do not be alarmed, this is not a grand physical plan for Europe. Neither is it an attempt to harmonise the planning systems of all the countries in the European Union (EU). Instead, it is a policy document agreed in 1999 at the EU's Informal Council of Ministers responsible for Spatial Planning. The document is based on the EU's aim of achieving balanced and sustainable development, in particular by strengthening economic and social cohesion. It has no legal force but seeks

FIGURE 2.1: *Hierarchy of planning policy and development plans*

EU: European Spatial Directive Perspective (ESDP)	
England	Wales
National level	
• New-style Planning Policy Statements (PPSs) • Old-style Planning Policy Guidance notes (PPGs) • Some policy guidance is set out in ministerial circulars or good practice guides	• Planning Guidance (Wales) • Ministerial Interim Planning Policy Statements (MIPPSs) • Technical Advice Notes (TANs) • WO/WAG circulars • Wales Spatial Plan
Regional level	
• Regional Spatial Strategies and planning guidance (including the Spatial Development Strategy for London)	• Non-statutory Regional Spatial Guidance produced by voluntary strategic planning groups, in partnership with local authorities
County/unitary authorities (NB all councils in Wales are unitary authorities)	
• Saved old-style Structure Plan and Unitary Development Plan policies • Minerals and waste development framework • Supplementary planning documents/guidance	• Saved old-style Structure Plans, Unitary Development Plans and Local Plans (to be phased out) • New-style Local Development Plans • Supplementary Planning Guidance
District/local level	
• Saved old-style Local Plan policies • New-style Local Development Frameworks (see Fig. 2.2) including Development Plan Documents • Supplementary planning documents/guidance	

better co-ordination between EU sectoral policies that have significant impacts, and between member states, their regions and cities. The European Spatial Development Perspective (ESDP) therefore sets out clear spatial development guidelines that transcend national boundaries.

National planning policy and guidance

National planning policies are issued by the UK government and the National Assembly for Wales on a range of issues. These guide not only the preparation of development plans and the policies within them, but also the way in which planning applications should be assessed.

In England, national policy is mainly expressed in the form of new-style Planning Policy Statements (PPSs), which are being introduced gradually to replace existing Planning Policy Guidance notes (PPGs). The new statements, which will be far fewer in number (in some cases several PPGs will be merged), are intended to be more streamlined and provide greater clarity. Each PPS or PPG sets out the national policy on a particular aspect of planning. For example, PPG2 deals with policy on Green Belts and PPS6 with planning for town centres. Current PPGs and PPSs are listed at Appendix A. However, just to complicate matters, some policy guidance (mainly older advice) is set out in departmental circulars, good practice guides or ministerial statements. In addition, in recent years the Department for Communities and Local Government (CLG) has disseminated some advice to local authorities in the form of so-called 'Dear Chief Planning Officer' letters. The CLG and Planning Portal websites include lists of relevant policy guidance, although older documents may not be available for download.

In Wales, the framework of current land-use policies is set out mainly in *Planning Policy Wales* (published by the National Assembly for Wales in March 2002 and amended by a series of Ministerial Interim Planning Policy Statements (MIPPSs) issued since 2005). *Planning Policy Wales* is supplemented by a companion guide, issued in 2006, and a series of topic-based Technical Advice Notes (TANs). These are also listed at Appendix A. Some policy and procedural advice is set out in circulars. Circular letters are also used to provide clarification of policy or procedure. Recent guidance may be viewed on the Welsh Assembly Government (WAG) website or via the Planning Portal. (Both the National Assembly for Wales and the WAG are involved in planning policy in Wales, but it is the National Assembly that is ultimately responsible. The WAG comprises the First Minister and the Cabinet, while the Assembly comprises the 60 Assembly Members – the Assembly delegates many of its powers to the First Minister and his Cabinet Ministers, but they remain answerable to the Assembly.)

Wales is the first and only UK nation to prepare a spatial plan. In the words of the National Assembly, *People, Places, Futures – The Wales Spatial Plan* (first published in 2004 and updated in 2008) 'sets out a direction of travel for Wales for the next 20 years, describing what is required to put Wales firmly on the path towards sustainable spatial development'. The Planning and Compulsory Purchase Act 2004 ('the 2004 Act') puts the plan on a statutory footing and requires it to be taken into account by all planning authorities when preparing their development plans. Visit www.wales.gov.uk for further details.

Current planning policies in both England and Wales place strong emphasis on sustainable patterns of development, mixed-use development, better design and the creation of sustainable communities (as defined in Section 1). The nations' respective governments are committed to delivering an 'urban renaissance', with greater re-use of previously developed or so-called 'brownfield' land – especially for housing – and the location of development where there is good access to public transport, services and facilities. All this, it is hoped, will reduce our dependence on the car, minimise the loss of greenfield land, and result in better living and working conditions in our towns and cities.

See also:
Place shaping,
page 9

Regional Spatial Strategies and Regional Planning Guidance

Under the old system, Regional Planning Guidance (RPG) was issued for each of the English regions, prepared on behalf of the Secretary of State by ad hoc teams under the control of each regional government office. Since the new provisions strengthening the role and importance of regional planning took effect in September 2004, all RPGs have become Regional Spatial Strategies (RSSs). These are also listed in Appendix A. The responsibility for revising RSSs rests with 'regional planning bodies' (RPBs). Following the government's decision to abolish regional assemblies from 2010, the unelected regional development agencies will be given new development and planning powers and will become RPBs.

Each RSS, incorporating a Regional Transport Strategy (RTS), provides a spatial framework to inform the preparation of Development Plan Documents (DPDs), Local Transport Plans (LTPs), and regional and sub-regional strategies and programmes that have a bearing on land-use activities. RSSs now carry statutory status and, together with the new DPDs, which must conform generally to the RSS, comprise part of the develop- ment plan.

> *See also: Meaning of 'development plan', page 13*

In England, the RSS provides a broad development strategy for the region for a period of around 15 to 20 years. It identifies the amount and distribution of new housing and employment and so forth, and takes into account matters such as:

- priorities for the environment, such as countryside and biodiversity protection, and
- transport, infrastructure, economic development, agriculture, minerals extrac- tion and waste treatment and disposal.

The spatial strategy of the RSS is set out on a key diagram. However, this does not identify specific sites suitable for development. That is the role of DPDs. An example of a published final RSS is the Yorkshire and Humber Plan (see www.gos.gov.uk/goyh/plan/regplan).

In Wales, while there is no statutory or national policy requirement to prepare RPGs, local planning authorities (LPAs) have collaborated and established volun- tary working arrangements to set strategic planning objectives and policies for their areas. These initiatives have informed the preparation of the Wales Spatial Plan and provide a strategic context for Local Development Plans (LDPs).

Planning Policy Statement 11: Regional Spatial Strategies (PPS11) sets out govern- ment policy and guidance on the preparation of RSSs within England. Under the Local Democracy, Economic Development and Construction Bill, it is proposed that in England regional economic strategies and RSSs will be combined into a new-style single strategy. The new arrangements will be explained in a revised version of PPS11, which is expected to be published in 2010.

Structure Plans

Structure Plans are old-style development plans prepared by and covering coun- ties and National Parks. They no longer feature in the post-2004 plan-making regime, unless their policies have been saved under transitional arrangements and so form part of the development plan.

Structure Plans took their lead from national and regional planning guidance, and set out key strategic policies, including the general amount and location of new housing, employment and other development. They provide the overall framework for Local Plans and normally deal with a period of 10 to 15 years. Structure Plans comprise a 'written statement' and a 'key diagram', illustrating the general policies.

Local Development Frameworks, Local Plans and Supplementary Planning Documents

Local Development Frameworks

Local Development Framework (LDF) is the non-statutory term for the *portfolio* or folder of Local Development Documents (LDDs) in England that comprise the spatial planning strategy for an LPA's area. LDDs were introduced as a result of the 2004 Act and is the collective term for the DPDs, which, once adopted, will replace the old system of Local, Structure and Unitary Development Plans (UDPs), as well as Supplementary Planning Documents (SPDs) and the Statement of Community Involvement (SCI). LDFs are intended to streamline the local planning process and be spatial, rather than purely land-use, plans. They set out a clear vision for an area, together with a realistic implementation strategy. The focus is on delivery, allocating sufficient land for new development to meet the needs identified in the RSS (including *The London Plan*), while also taking account of views on the preferred location for such development. The new system is designed so that local authorities can decide which combination of documents best suits their circumstances. The ability to produce various documents rather than one plan is intended to make it easier to keep policies and proposals up to date. Reforms made in 2008 have reduced the complexity and number of DPDs and given LPAs greater flexibility in deciding which DPDs to prepare.

See also: Introduction and explanation of 'spatial planning', page 5

DPDs include:

- a mandatory *Core Strategy*, setting out the spatial vision, spatial objectives and core policies of the planning authority's area over a lifespan of 15 years or more; since 2008, it may also allocate strategic sites

- other DPDs (optional), for example to provide additional detail, or to allocate non-strategic sites that would not be suitable for inclusion within the Core Strategy
- a *Proposals Map*, illustrating site allocations and the areas to which specific policies apply, including flood risk zones and areas to be protected, such as Green Belts and conservation areas
- *Area Action Plans*, if appropriate, to focus on specific areas where significant change or conservation is needed, such as in growth and regeneration areas.

For an example of an adopted Core Strategy DPD and a Development Policies DPD, prepared under the pre-2008 procedures, together with an Allocations DPD, see Hambleton District Council's website.

In addition to the DPDs listed above, the LDF portfolio will contain:

- a mandatory Local Development Scheme (LDS), setting out details of each of the DPDs to be produced and the timescales and arrangements for production
- an SCI, specifying how the authority intends to involve communities and stakeholders in the DPD preparation process
- an Annual Monitoring Report (AMR), setting out progress on producing DPDs and implementing policies
- SPDs, providing supplementary guidance on policies in the DPDs (optional) – these do not form part of the development plan or are subject to independent examination
- any Local Development Orders (LDOs) and/or Simplified Planning Zones (SPZs) that have been adopted (see Section 5, *Is permission necessary?*, page 54, for explanations of these terms).

Together with the RSS, to which they must conform generally, the DPDs comprise the development plan for the purposes of section 38(6) of the 2004 Act.

Figure 2.2 (page 26) shows the new plan-making regime and the contents of an LDF at a glance. The Planning Portal also includes a visual guide to LDFs.

Wales

In Wales, new-style LDPs are being prepared to replace existing UDPs, Structure Plans and Local Plans. These are simpler, more concise documents than the previous or current UDPs and focus on the planning authority's objectives for the use and development of land in its area, and the general policies for implementing them. They include specific allocations and detailed proposals,

FIGURE 2.2: *Contents of a local development framework*

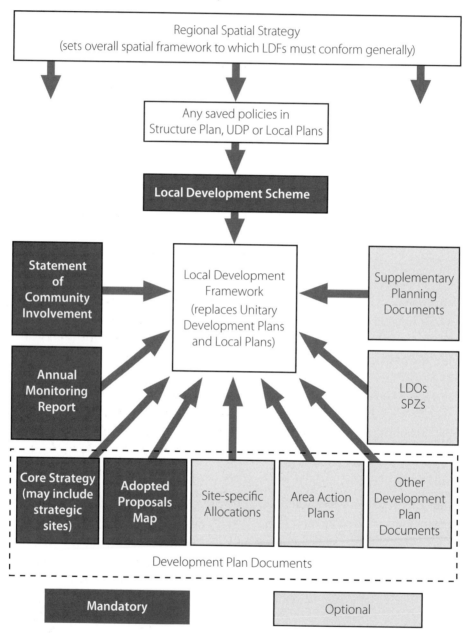

Source: adapted from *Creating Local Development Frameworks: A Companion Guide to PPS12*, ODPM, 2004, and updated to accord with changes made in 2008.

which are illustrated on a proposals map. Unlike the current UDPs, they are not split into two parts. LDPs need to be informed by a Sustainability Appraisal (SA) and be prepared in accordance with a Community Involvement Scheme (CIS) and a timetable to be agreed between each planning authority and the WAG.

Old-style Local Plans

In a very few areas, old-style Local Plans, prepared by and covering district council areas and some unitary and National Park authorities, may still be close to being completed under transitional provisions. Others may have been largely saved until superseded by new-style development documents in accordance with directions issued by the Secretary of State. Such old-style Local Plans set out local planning policies that work up in detail the broad strategy of the Structure Plan (to which they must generally conform), to guide day-to-day planning decisions. They also identify specific sites for development.

A Local Plan normally covers a period of about ten years and includes a written statement, which contains the plan's policies and proposals with reasoned justification, and a 'proposals map' on an Ordnance Survey base.

Supplementary Planning Guidance/Documents

Many local planning authorities have prepared Supplementary Planning Guidance (SPG) to expand upon development plan policy. Examples might include a 'planning brief' for a specific site, explaining how it should be developed; a 'design guide' for householder developments, residential development or shopfronts; a Village Design Statement; or advice on a particular topic, such as developer contributions or affordable housing. These documents are issued for guidance only. SPG is replaced under the new plan-making regime by SPDs, which will form part of the LDF for an area. Nevertheless, while subject to community involvement, SPDs are not independently examined and, as with old-style SPG, do not comprise part of the statutory development plan. They are thus given less weight in the decision-making process.

Further information

In England, further information is set out in *Planning Policy Statement 12: Local Spatial Planning* (PPS12) (2008) and in the Planning Advisory Service's online

Plan Making Manual – visit www.pas.gov.uk. In Wales, see the WAG's *Local Development Plan Manual* and its publication *Planning Your Community: A guide to Local Development Plans* (both issued in 2006).

Minerals and waste local plans

In England, minerals and waste DPDs should be contained within a separate minerals and waste development framework and continue to be prepared by counties, National Parks and some unitary authorities. They will set out policies for the control and location of mineral workings and the disposal of waste.

Wales is divided into three regional waste planning areas. Each has a non-statutory regional waste plan that provides a land-use planning framework for the region, and which will inform the preparation of LDPs.

Unitary Development Plans

UDPs, prepared by metropolitan district and unitary local authorities (including those in Wales), are old-style plans that combine the Structure Plan and the Local Plan functions. They are split into two parts. Part I contains the strategic policies, Part II sets out the detailed policies and proposals. They normally cover a period of ten years, and have a 'written statement' and 'proposals map'. Under transitional arrangements, some UDP policies have been saved and thus continue to have statutory force until superseded by DPDs or LDPs. Some emerging UDPs that had already reached the statutory deposit stage at the time the 2004 Act took effect have been allowed to be completed under modified procedures.

The Spatial Development Strategy for London

This is similar to an RSS. The Spatial Development Strategy for London, published in February 2004 under the title *The London Plan*, is a spatial development strategy prepared by the Mayor of London. It replaces the previous strategic planning guidance for London (known as RPG3), issued by the Secretary of State. Alterations to the Plan's housing provision targets and waste and minerals policies were published in December 2006, and are formally part of the London Plan.

SUMMARY

- The European Spatial Development Perspective sets out clear spatial development guidelines for EU member states that transcend national boundaries, but it has no legal force.
- Planning policies for England are issued by the UK government, and policies for Wales by the National Assembly for Wales.
- Regional Spatial Strategies (RSSs) are the highest level of development strategy within an English region (intended to cover a period of 15 to 20 years) and replace the previous Regional Planning Guidance.
- The regional spatial framework set by the RSS is worked up in greater detail and applied through Development Plan Documents (DPDs). The RSS and the DPDs together form the development plan.
- 'Local Development Framework' (LDF) refers to a portfolio of Local Development Documents that comprise the spatial planning strategy for a local planning authority's area, setting out the vision for an area and a realistic implementation strategy. LDFs replace the previous system of Local, Structure and Unitary Development Plans.
- Local planning authorities may have also produced Supplementary Planning Guidance, although such documents are non-statutory and are being replaced by Supplementary Planning Documents.
- Transitional arrangements are still in place, so that some policies from old-style development plans are subject to a saving direction and thus continue to have statutory force, while a very few old-style development plans that were well advanced at the time the 2004 Act took effect may still remain to be completed.

Section 3
Special designations and related controls

In this Section:

- *National Parks*
- *Areas of Outstanding Natural Beauty*
- *Green Belts*
- *Nature conservation sites*
- *Historic and archaeological interests*
- *Reform of the heritage protection regime*

In recognition of their special interest, qualities or role, government agencies and local planning authorities (LPAs) have designated certain areas of countryside, townscape, individual buildings or other features as being worthy of particular protection. Many of these are subject to additional statutory controls and procedures. This Section lists the principal types of special designation.

National Parks

In England, National Parks are designated by Natural England (formerly known as the Countryside Agency, and, prior to that, the Countryside Commission) under the National Parks and Access to the Countryside Act 1949, subject to confirmation by the Secretary of State. National Park designation is the highest form of landscape protection. In Wales, responsibility for National Parks lies with the Countryside Council for Wales (CCW).

The main statutory purposes of National Parks include the conservation and enhancement of their natural beauty, wildlife and cultural heritage. The relevant National Park authorities also have a statutory duty to promote opportunities for public understanding and enjoyment of the National Parks' special qualities, and to foster the economic and social well-being of their local communities. In the event of conflict between these different duties, priority is given to conservation. In addition to influencing the consideration of planning applications, especially for major developments, certain permitted development rights are restricted in National Parks.

On 1 March 2005, the New Forest was designated as a National Park in England, and this was joined on 31 March 2009 by the South Downs. These bring the total number of National Parks in England to ten, with a further three in Wales.

(Refer to Natural England's website for details: www.naturalengland.org.uk)

Areas of Outstanding Natural Beauty

Areas of Outstanding Natural Beauty (AONBs) are designated in much the same way as National Parks, under the same legislation, and are of equal importance in terms of their landscape and scenic beauty. Natural England and CCW are responsible for formally designating AONBs and for advising on policies for their protection. The main purpose of AONB designation is the conservation of their natural beauty, so planning decisions will favour this. However, regard must also be had to the needs of agriculture, forestry and other uses, and to the economic and social well-being of the area. However, unlike National Parks, the promotion of recreation is not an objective of designation.

There are 40 AONBs in England and Wales (35 wholly in England, four wholly in Wales and one that straddles the border). In total they cover about 18 per cent of the countryside in England and Wales.

Permitted development rights are reduced in AONBs (see Section 5, *Permitted development*, page 55).

Green Belts

Green Belts cover about 13 per cent of England (about the same as built-up areas) and are established through development plans (old-style Structure Plans previously dealing with their general extent, with Local Plans defining the boundaries). Many of England's larger towns and cities are surrounded by Green Belt land. At present, there are no Green Belts in Wales, which so far has operated a broadly similar system of green wedges or barriers. However, a Green Belt is proposed between Cardiff and Newport in an emerging Local Development Plan.

Relevant guidance for England is set out in *Planning Policy Guidance 2: Green Belts* (PPG2) (1995). This explains that Green Belts have five purposes:

- To check the unrestricted sprawl of large built-up areas.
- To prevent neighbouring towns from merging into one another.
- To assist in safeguarding the countryside from encroachment.
- To preserve the setting and special character of historic towns.
- To assist urban regeneration by encouraging the recycling of derelict and other urban land.

It should be noted that Green Belts are entirely functional; their designation is not a reflection of their landscape quality. An essential characteristic of Green Belts is their openness. In the main, therefore, development within them is prohibited – there is a presumption against so-called 'inappropriate development', which should not be permitted except in 'very special circumstances'. The courts have held that when assessing this, the words 'very special' must be given their ordinary and natural meaning. The circumstances must be not merely special in the sense of unusual or exceptional, but *very special*.

PPG2 advises that development will be inappropriate unless it is for certain defined purposes. These include:

- agriculture and forestry (unless permitted development rights have been withdrawn)
- essential facilities for sport and outdoor recreation, for cemeteries and for other uses of land which preserve the openness of the Green Belt and which do not conflict with the purposes of including land in it
- limited extension, alteration or replacement of existing dwellings
- limited infilling in existing villages (either 'washed over' or 'inset', that is, excluded from the Green Belt) and limited affordable housing for local community needs under development plan policies
- limited infilling or redevelopment of major existing developed sites identified in adopted Local Plans, which meet certain criteria
- the reuse of buildings where (in summary): the new use would not have a materially greater impact than the present use on the openness of the

Green Belt and the purposes of including land in it; there is strict control over any extensions or associated development, such as parking; the buildings are of permanent and substantial construction and are capable of conversion without major or complete reconstruction; and the form, bulk and general design of the buildings are in keeping with their surroundings.

An important feature of Green Belts is their permanence, although their boundaries may be reviewed periodically and altered in exceptional circumstances.

In accordance with The Town and Country Planning (Consultation) (England) Direction 2009 (CLG Circular 02/2009), planning applications for 'inappropriate development' of certain types and scale in the Green Belt that LPAs are minded to approve must first be referred to the Secretary of State so that they may consider whether to call in the more significant and harmful development proposals in the Green Belt for their own determination, following a public inquiry.

Guidance on green wedges and Green Belts in Wales is set out in *Planning Policy Wales* (NAW, 2002).

Nature conservation sites

Essentially, nature conservation sites may be divided into those that are statutory designations, which are Sites of Special Scientific Interest (SSSIs), and those that are not, such as local nature reserves or 'sites of importance for nature conservation' which are established by a variety of private and public bodies (including LPAs). All sites of national and international importance, such as so-called 'European sites' (Ramsar sites, Special Protection Areas and Special Areas of Conservation) are SSSIs and are the responsibility of Natural England. Natural England must be consulted on any planning application that would affect an SSSI.

Further information on the complex relationship between planning control and nature conservation is given in, for England, *Planning Policy Statement 9: Biodiversity and Geological Conservation* (PPS9), the accompanying Good Practice Guide and *ODPM Circular 06/2005: Biodiversity and Geological Conservation – Statutory obligations and their impact within the planning system* (August 2005). For Wales, see *Technical Advice Note 5: Nature Conservation and Planning* (TAN5).

Historic and archaeological interests

In addition to normal planning controls, the Planning (Listed Buildings and Conservation Areas) Act 1990 provides special controls for the protection of certain historic buildings and designated conservation areas.

Listed buildings

From time to time, buildings of special architectural or historic interest may be 'listed' (that is, added to a statutory list approved by the Secretary of State or National Assembly). The effect of this is to require specific consent ('listed building consent') for any demolition, or for internal or external works that would *affect the special interest of a listed building*. This is regardless of whether any physical feature affected is mentioned in the list description, or whether any planning permission is also necessary for the proposed works. The need for such consent may also extend to buildings or other structures attached to or within the curtilage of a listed building (that is, the area of land associated with the building). There are a number of tests as to whether an object or structure falls within a curtilage for the purposes of listed building control and these are explained in *Planning Policy Guidance 15: Planning and the Historic Environment* (PPG15). However, listed building consent is not normally required for repairs (although these should always be discussed with the LPA beforehand).

Listed buildings are graded according to their relative importance:

• Grade I: buildings of exceptional interest (about 2 per cent).
• Grade II*: more than average special interest, but not outstanding (about 4 per cent). Often these will have fine interiors or strong historical associations.
• Grade II: buildings of special architectural or historic interest that warrant every effort being made to preserve them (about 94 per cent).

The statutory list (and accompanying maps) may be inspected at LPA offices. The National Monuments Record, the national public archive of English Heritage, provides a range of very helpful services, some of which are free (see www.english-heritage.org.uk). In Wales, the equivalent body is CADW (Welsh Historic Monuments).

Since 1 April 2005 English Heritage has been responsible for the administration of the listing system within England.

Conservation areas

Conservation areas are designated by LPAs and are 'areas of special architectural or historic interest, the character or appearance of which it is desirable to preserve or enhance'. Over 9000 conservation areas have been designated in accordance with guidelines issued by the government and English Heritage/CADW. The main consideration is the quality and interest of the area rather than that of individual buildings, although conservation areas will, of course, often include a high proportion of listed buildings. Although there is no statutory requirement to do so, it is normal practice for planning authorities to consult residents and others affected before making a conservation area. Increasingly, this is done as part of the process of making a new development plan.

Development within conservation areas is not ruled out. However, when considering applications within a conservation area, decision-makers have a statutory duty to pay special attention to the desirability of preserving or enhancing the area's character or appearance. The courts have held that this does not mean that all developments must *positively* 'preserve or enhance', merely that the character and appearance of a conservation area should not be harmed by the proposed development (*South Lakeland District Council v. Secretary of State for the Environment and Carlisle Diocesan Parsonages Board* [1992] 2 WLR 204).

Permitted development rights are reduced within conservation areas, and in some cases they may be removed altogether by a so-called 'article 4 direction'. There are also special controls over trees and over the display of advertisements. In addition, conservation area consent is required for most demolition works. We say more about procedures within conservation areas in Section 5, *Listed building and conservation area consent* (page 64).

Scheduled monuments and areas of archaeological importance

The Ancient Monuments and Archaeological Areas Act 1979, as amended, deals with controls over the carrying out of works to a scheduled monument and with the designation of 'areas of archaeological importance'. Where development would damage or alter a scheduled monument, it is first necessary to apply to the Secretary of State (English Heritage) for Scheduled Monument Consent. The procedure for this is similar to that for called-in planning applications, prompting a public inquiry or hearing so that interested parties can express their views. Consent may be granted, with or without conditions, or refused.

A consent will lapse after five years, unless the works have been carried out or started.

Areas of archaeological importance have been designated in certain historic centres (including, for example, Chester and York). However, relevant statutory powers are intended to allow time for 'rescue archaeology', investigation and recording, rather than preventing damage to archaeological interests.

Other heritage designations

Other heritage designations include:

- World Heritage Sites
- Heritage Coasts
- Historic Parks and Gardens
- Historic Battlefields.

Further information

For England, further information on archaeological interests is currently set out in *Planning Policy Guidance 16: Archaeology and Planning* (PPG16). In Wales, *WO Circular 60/96: Planning and the Historic Environment: Archaeology* contains similar guidance.

Further information on listed buildings, conservation areas and other heritage assets is set out in PPG15 (for England, but see below) and in *WO Circular 61/ 96: Planning and the Historic Environment: Historic Buildings and Conservation Areas* (for Wales). *CLG Circular 07/2009* applies to England only and provides policy guidance on the protection of World Heritage Sites.

Reform of the heritage protection regime

In March 2007, the Department for Culture, Media and Sport (DCMS) and the Welsh Assembly Government published a joint White Paper, *Heritage Protection for the 21st Century*, which proposed various changes to the heritage protection regime. Some of these were included in CLG Circular 01/2007, which sets out revised principles for the selection of listed buildings (replacing paragraphs 6.1 to 6.40 of PPG15). Others were carried forward into a draft Heritage Protection Bill, which was published in April 2008. The draft bill contained provisions to unify the designation and consent regimes for what were described as 'terrestrial heritage assets' or 'registered heritage structures' (listed buildings and scheduled ancient monuments), and to transfer responsibility for their designation (to be renamed 'registration') in England from the Secretary of State to English Heritage. Under the new regime, a single 'heritage asset consent' (HAC) would replace the existing listed building consent, scheduled monument consent and conservation area consent requirements. In addition, the bill provided for a system of appeals against or reviews of registration decisions in both England and Wales.

The most controversial elements of the bill related to conservation areas. It was proposed that these be designated as currently, except that it would also be possible to designate a conservation area on the basis of special archaeological and artistic interest. However, it was also proposed to reverse the outcome of the *South Lakeland* judgment (see above), in which it was held that section 72 of the Planning (Listed Buildings and Conservation Areas) Act 1990 does not require LPAs to insist that developments are beneficial to conservation areas, merely that they do not harm them. Instead, it was proposed that where a change does not benefit (enhance) the conservation area, it would not be considered to be appropriate. In addition, DCMS announced its intention to reverse the judgment in *Shimizu (UK) Ltd v. Westminster City Council* [1997] 1 WLR 168, which had established that demolition of only part of an unlisted building in a conservation area does not need conservation area consent, because it is considered to be an alteration.

Although the draft bill has been put on hold, the government is pressing ahead with many of its proposed reforms. In collaboration with DCMS and English Heritage, in July 2009 CLG published a draft new PPS on the historic environment, which will replace current guidance for the historic environment in PPG15 and PPG16. The draft PPS builds on the changes proposed in the 2007 White Paper. It takes an integrated approach to buildings and archaeology, and defines the historic environment in terms of heritage assets to be conserved and, where appropriate, enhanced in accordance with a set of common principles in proportion to their significance (defined in terms of historic, archaeological, architectural or artistic interest). Draft practice guidance to support the policy principles in the draft PPS has been prepared by English Heritage (see www.english-heritage.org.uk/pps).

To keep up to date on progress with the heritage protection reform programme, visit the English Heritage website or go to the DCMS website at: www.culture.gov.uk/what_we_do/historic_environment/5635.aspx

---

SUMMARY

- You must be aware of the special controls and procedures that apply to certain designated areas and buildings. The statutory controls vary between designations, and watch out for differences between English and Welsh guidance.
- Ensure that you are aware of the restrictions imposed by listed building status, and understand the implications of conservation areas.
- In England, the heritage protection regime is in the process of reform. Monitor the DCMS and English Heritage websites for progress.

Section 4
Getting involved in policy formulation

In this Section:

- *Grow your role!*
- *Key involvement stages in plan-making*
- *Development Plan Documents*
- *Supplementary Planning Documents*
- *Transitional arrangements*
- *Sustainable Community Strategies*
- *Strategic Housing Land Availability Assessments*

Grow your role!

Architect Michael Wildblood has said:

> The one area where architects excel over all others is in the conceptual design of buildings and, whether we like it or not, the framework for translating these skills into increased value for our clients is to 'grow' their role in the planning process.

> I believe that if architects could increase their skills in influencing the drawing up of development plans, in relating their designs to the policies of these plans and central government advice, and in being able to write about them as well as draw them (design statements and public inquiry/written reps evidence), we would be a more respected profession.

So, how can you 'grow your role' in the plan-making process?

Long gone are the days when the first you heard that a land-use plan had even been prepared was when the local authority published it and announced that it had been adopted. Over the years, planning authorities have experimented with ways to involve everyone whose lives would be affected by a new plan and let them have their say in its preparation. Thus, the involvement of individuals, communities and the whole gamut of interest groups – including industry and commerce – has been developed and written into successive government land-use plan-making legislation. Today, no one can truthfully say that there has been no opportunity in the development policy and plan-making process when their views could be expressed and be taken into account.

An important feature of the new plan-making regime is that it offers strengthened opportunities for what the government calls 'community and stakeholder involvement'. This is now front-loaded, meaning that more active involvement is possible much earlier in the plan-preparation process to influence the content of an emerging plan and, in particular, to put forward sites for consideration for development.

The government's objectives for increased public participation were set out in its paper *Community Involvement in Planning*, published by the Office of the Deputy Prime Minister (ODPM) in February 2004 (Annex A of the paper contains a useful summary of the opportunities, which are largely still relevant).

Key involvement stages in plan-making

'Constant change is the steady state.' This is true for many development plans and the policies embedded in them, be they at national, regional or local level. New plans and guidance are drawn up at the same time that others are being reviewed and updated. Goalposts are moved. So, in your clients' interests as well as your own, you should not only remain vigilant but also be proactive.

If any of your clients has not already commissioned a planning consultant to look after their property interests (and this is a specialist job), then as soon as the first draft proposals or preferred options of any Development Plan Document (DPD) are published, it is vital that you study them carefully to check whether your client's land-use planning interests are affected. You might find that it is proposed to change the use of land currently earmarked for development to another use that is far less acceptable to your client. For example, when reviewing existing plans, in recent years many planning authorities have sought to remove certain existing greenfield allocations or sites that do not perform well in sustainability terms. You may also discover that it is proposed to change or tighten up more general policies which, although not site-specific, might indirectly not be in the best interests of either yourself, as a practitioner, or your current or prospective clients.

You may, of course, wish to influence the contents of an emerging plan to actively *promote* a particular development, or to secure more favourable policies or circumstances in advance of any application for permission.

Traditionally, the process of plan-making, at whatever level, has been drawn out over several years, with lengthy intervals between successive stages. But while anyone wishing to get involved should not enter into the process lightly and should be prepared for a long haul, the revised new regime – with its emphasis on speedier plan preparation – should make active participation easier to sustain.

Be aware also of the opportunities for involvement in the preparation of Sustainable Community Strategies (SCSs) and, in particular, Strategic Housing Land Availability Assessments (SHLAAs), which local authorities are required to prepare. Brief discussions of these are included at the end of this Section.

National and regional levels

There are a number of opportunities for feeding in ideas and making your views known when change is in the air. At national level, you can promote your ideas by responding constructively to consultation papers and draft guidance, including emerging replacement Planning Policy Statements. These are published on the Department for Communities and Local Government (CLG) and National Assembly for Wales websites and are normally accompanied by a press release highlighting the key changes. Usually, a period of at least 12 weeks is given for public comment.

At regional level, you can do the same by commenting on a draft revised Regional Spatial Strategy (RSS). The main stages at which you can do this are:

• the project plan, which will include the objectives of the revision, the areas to be covered and the timetable for preparing the RSS
• the draft strategic options and policies, and subsequent submission of the draft revision to the Secretary of State

- its public scrutiny at the Examination in Public (EiP) before an independent panel
- the Secretary of State's proposed changes to the draft revision following receipt of the report of the EiP panel.

Figure 4.1 (page 45) summarises the key stages in the RSS review process.

However, it will normally be at the local level – where key decisions are made on the distribution of new development, the formulation of development management policies and the allocation of specific sites – that architects will probably most want to get involved in the plan-making process.

Local level – Development Plan Documents

The starting point is to check the planning authority's Local Development Scheme (LDS), as this will tell you when you can expect opportunities to get involved in the plan-making process. The LDS is a programme that each planning authority is required to publish on its website and keep updated, setting out the authority's intentions for preparing its Local Development Framework (LDF).

The LDS will give you the details of each of the DPDs to be produced, their order of priority, and the timescales and arrangements for their production. It will also tell you the local authority's planning policies for a particular place or issue and the status of those policies. Although there is no longer any requirement to do so, the LDS may also give details of any existing or proposed Supplementary Planning Documents. The LDS is not subject to independent examination or public consultation.

Planning authorities must also publish a Statement of Community Involvement (SCI), explaining to local communities and stakeholders how they will be involved in the preparation of DPDs and the steps that authorities will take to facilitate this. The SCI, which is itself subject to public consultation, also covers other planning activities, including the local planning authority's (LPA) approach to pre-application discussions and arrangements for involving the community in planning applications and planning obligations.

So, a perusal of these two important documents will enable you to establish exactly what plans an authority has in store and how you can set about trying to influence their contents.

FIGURE 4.1: *Main stages in the RSS revision process (shaded boxes denote opportunities for public involvement)*

Stage 1
Identification of issues for revision and preparation of a draft Project Plan and Statement of Public Participation (up to 4 months)

Stage 2
Preparation of initial strategic options and policies, assessment of impacts and development of draft RSS revision, involving public (up to 12 months)

Stage 3
Publication of draft RSS and Sustainability Appraisal for formal consultation, following submission to Secretary of State (SoS) (up to 3½ months)

Stage 4
Testing of the submitted draft RSS revision at examination-in-public before independent panel appointed by SoS, following analysis of representations received (5–6½ months)

Stage 5
Publication of panel report to SoS (2–3 months)

Stage 6
Publication of changes proposed by SoS and subsequent consultation (up to 6 months)

Stage 7
Final RSS approved and issued by SoS (c. 2½–3 years from start of process)

Source: adapted from *Planning Policy Statement 11: Regional Spatial Strategies*, ODPM, 2004.

"The most important DPD is the Core Strategy"

The most important DPD is the Core Strategy. Following revised procedures, this may contain strategic sites and can be the only DPD that an LPA prepares. It may also extend beyond the planning authority's boundary and be prepared jointly with other authorities. In line with the overarching SCS, the Core Strategy sets out the long-term vision and strategic priorities for the development of a local area.

However, in many cases you may also need to try to influence the content of a subsequent DPD, such as one that makes specific site allocations or sets out detailed policies. Planning authorities have been given more flexibility in deciding what process they will adopt to enable them to meet their legal obligations on plan-making and on who, when and for how long to consult when doing this. Practice will therefore vary, so the following is just a guide.

There are four main stages in preparing a DPD:

- pre-production
- production
- examination
- adoption.

Pre-production stage

At this stage, the main activities are carrying out survey work and gathering evidence, resulting in a decision to include a DPD in the LDS. The intention is for the authority to come to a thorough understanding of current and future local issues and needs, based on material collected by relevant organisations, community interest groups and its own original research.

Production stage

This is obviously the stage when you could have the greatest influence. Amended regulations and guidance issued in 2008 have streamlined plan preparation, resulting in the removal of any formal requirement to consult on any 'issues and options' and 'preferred options' stages, in favour of a continuous process of community engagement. Nevertheless, since it is up to the LPA to decide how it wishes to do this, it may still publish a preferred options or similar report. But whatever form the consultation may take, it is likely to be early in the process, so you should be alert to this. It must also be carried out in accordance with the SCI and any representations made must be taken into account.

The next step is the publication of the DPD, which some mistakenly call a draft plan. This will be subject to a minimum of six weeks' consultation, prior to its submission to the Secretary of State for independent public examination. At this mandatory stage in the process, representations on the 'soundness' of the DPD can be made, and these will be taken into account during the examination. If the representations made are so significant that they require a major rewrite of the plan, the LPA may decide to withdraw the DPD and submit an amended version at a later date.

The DPD is submitted to the Secretary of State with a final Sustainability Appraisal (SA), including a Strategic Environmental Assessment (SEA) required by European Directive 2001/42/EC, which will also have been the subject of a staged con-sultation process. The purpose of the SA is to appraise the social, environmental and economic effects of the submitted DPD, to ensure that it accords with the principles of sustainable development. Further information on this is set out in the ODPM publication *Sustainability Appraisal of Regional Spatial Strategies and Local Development Documents* (November 2005).

If you are seeking to make a significant change to the emerging DPD – such as arguing for additional or alternative sites to be included or for the boundary of a site identified in the submitted document to be modified in some way – it is vital that you do so at every available opportunity given by the LPA. However, do bear in mind that if you want to participate in the public examination, you must lodge your representations before the requisite deadline on the formal consultation on the published DPD, since only those lodged at this stage and which are judged to be 'duly made' are eligible to be considered during the examination. The planning authority will publish a standard form for representa-tions on its website.

When seeking a change, you should be as specific as possible about what it is that you would like to see, for example by identifying clearly on an extract from the proposals map the precise change, such as any new site and its proposed use. It is also possible that you might wish to support some aspect of the emerging DPD, and such representations can be considered at the examination stage.

Examination

Unlike under the old system, planning authorities no longer publish pre-examination changes, other than in exceptional circumstances. An independent inspector appointed by the Secretary of State will conduct the examination, the purpose of which will be to consider whether the submitted DPD complies with legal requirements and is sound when judged against three tests of soundness. These tests are whether the planning document is:

- justified – that is, founded on a robust and credible evidence base and the most appropriate strategy when considered against reasonable alternatives
- effective – meaning that it is deliverable, flexible and able to be monitored, and
- consistent with national planning policy.

The government expects that the majority of representations will be considered by way of written representations and points out that these are treated as equally important as those 'heard' by the inspector. Only those seeking a change to the DPD have a right to be heard. This may take the form of an informal 'round table' discussion or a hearing. Alternatively, where there are strongly opposed views that may need to be tested and legal representation is required, a more formal hearing may be necessary. The Planning Inspectorate has published a brief guide to examining DPDs on its website, together with more detailed information in *Development Plans Examination – A guide to the process of assessing the soundness of development plan documents* (November 2005).

If you are promoting a site that has been omitted from the published DPD, be aware that you may need to gain in-depth knowledge of every background research document commissioned by the LPA. You will also have to study any submissions putting forward rival sites – competing parties may well have attacked your client's proposals in their own representations!

Adoption and the inspector's binding report

After the examination, the inspector will produce a report that is binding upon the planning authority. This differs from the procedure under the old system, where the inspector was only able to make a set of recommendations and the planning authority was not obliged to accept them (although, unless it had good reason not to do so, it invariably did). The inspector's report will explain how the DPD and the proposals map must be changed, or identify matters that require further consideration, and give reasons for so doing.

Unless the Secretary of State intervenes, the planning authority must adopt the submitted development plan as changed by the inspector's binding report.

Annual Monitoring Report

The Annual Monitoring Report (AMR) is a mandatory report submitted to the Secretary of State by the LPA to assess the progress and the effectiveness of an LDF. The AMR sets out:

- how the LPA is performing against the timescales and milestones set out in its LDS
- information on the extent to which policies in the LDF are being achieved
- advice on the need to update the LDS.

The AMR therefore provides a lot of useful background information, including that on meeting housing requirements (see also discussion on Strategic Housing Land Availability Assessments, below).

Figure 4.2 (page 50) shows the main stages in the preparation of a DPD.

Supplementary Planning Documents

Supplementary Planning Documents (SPDs) replace Supplementary Planning Guidance (SPG) produced previously by planning authorities. While not having development plan status, SPDs are used to expand policy or provide further detail to policies in DPDs. The process for their preparation is broadly similar to that for a DPD. However, while they will be informed by extensive community involvement, there is no independent examination stage to test that they are sound or need for them to be subject to sustainability appraisal.

Transitional arrangements

A very small number of emerging old-style development plans may currently be close to completion. Opportunities for further representations on such plans will now be extremely limited.

FIGURE 4.2: *Main stages in preparing a Development Plan Document (DPD)*

Pre-production	Evidence gathering

- -

Production — Preparation of Issues and Options/Preferred Option Report (non-statutory) with continuous consultation with the community/stakeholders, and consideration of representations received. Practice will vary

Preparation of DPD for submission to SoS

6-week minimum formal consultation on submission of DPD

Depending on representations received, DPD may be withdrawn to be rewritten or submitted to SoS

- -

Examination — Pre-examination meeting

Independent examination by Planning Inspectorate on submitted DPD's soundness

Inspector's binding report

- -

Adoption — Adoption of DPD

Monitoring and review

Sustainability Appraisal (SA), including Strategic Environmental Assessment (SEA)

Source: adapted from *Planning Policy Statement 12: Local Development Frameworks*, ODPM 2004, and updated to accord with changes made in 2008.

Sustainable Community Strategies

The Local Government Act 2000 introduced the concept of 'community strategies', subsequently renamed as 'sustainable community strategies', as a way of:

> promoting or improving the economic, social and environmental well-being of their areas and contributing to the achievement of sustainable development in the United Kingdom.

The duty was placed on 'principal' local authorities to each prepare its own strategy, although this may be passed to Local Strategic Partnerships, which include local authority representatives. Through the SCS, authorities are expected to set out the strategic vision for a place – linked to regional strategies – and to co-ordinate the actions of local public, private, voluntary and community sectors on cross-cutting issues. The SCS provides a key community input into the preparation by the LPA of its Core Strategy, which must align with the SCS's priorities for an area. So here is another great opportunity for members of the architectural profession to get themselves positively involved in 'growing their role' and, in turn, influence outcomes in the statutory spatial planning process.

For further information, see *Preparing Community Strategies: Government guidance to local authorities* (ODPM, December 1999) and *PPS12: Local Spatial Planning* (2008), both published on the CLG website, and *Local Vision: Statutory guidance from the Welsh Assembly Government on developing and delivering community strategies* (WAG, 2008).

Strategic Housing Land Availability Assessments

In accordance with PPS3, these assessments must be carried out by English LPAs in order to identify land for housing and to assess the deliverability and developability of sites. The SHLAA involves a partnership approach with various stakeholders, including house builders. Since the SHLAA is an important evidence source to inform plan-making, especially an authority's Core Strategy, you and your clients should take whatever opportunities arise to comment on or put forward development sites for consideration. The SHLAA is not a one-off study, but should be an integral part of the LPA's annual monitoring of its LDF. Further information is set out in PPS3 and in *Strategic Housing Land Availability Assessments: Practice guidance*, published by CLG in 2007.

SUMMARY

- There are many opportunities for you, as an architect, to become involved in influencing planning policy – at national, regional and local levels.
- At a national level, be prepared to respond to government consultation and draft guidance documents – check the CLG and WAG websites regularly for new documents.
- At a regional level, comment on drafts of the Regional Spatial Strategy.
- The Local Development Framework and Development Plan Documents offer the greatest opportunities for influencing planning policy, so check your planning authority's Local Development Scheme to identify where you can get involved in the plan-making process.
- You should be prepared to review emerging Development Plan Documents to check whether your clients' land-use interests are affected. Be prepared to actively support proposals as well as object to those not in your clients' interests, and to put forward new proposals.
- Sustainable Community Strategies offer another opportunity for you to 'grow your role'. Where appropriate, you should also provide an input into the LPA's Strategic Housing Land Availability Assessment, when this is being prepared.

Section 5
Applications for planning permission or other consent

In this Section:

- *Is permission necessary?*
- *Who can apply?*
- *Who processes planning applications?*
- *Main types of application*
- *Preparing and submitting planning applications*
- *What happens to your application and what should you do?*
- *Negotiations and tactics*
- *Decision notices*
- *Planning conditions*
- *Planning obligations, developer contributions and 'planning gain'*

As an architect, your day-to-day dealings with planning authorities will most likely mean the submission of applications and trying to secure permission for your proposals. It is therefore vital that you understand the processes and the people involved, and where to look for extra guidance. Of course, you should not confuse the role of the planning system with that of the entirely separate Building Regulations regime or forget that the achievement of planning permission does not override the need for Building Regulations approval or any other consent that may be required.

Is permission necessary?

Definition of development

When considering whether planning permission is necessary, it is perhaps helpful to understand the legal definition of 'development'. Section 55 of the Town and Country Planning Act 1990 ('the 1990 Act') defines development for which planning permission is required as:

> the carrying out of building, engineering, mining or other operations in, on, over or under land, or the making of any material change in the use of any buildings or other land.

The definition essentially has two parts:

- operational development
- changes of use.

For the purposes of the 1990 Act, operational development includes:

- demolition of buildings
- rebuilding
- structural alterations of or additions to buildings
- 'other operations normally undertaken by a person carrying on business as a builder'.

Or, as the courts have put it: 'activities which result in some physical alteration to the land, which has some degree of permanence'. The definition of development does not extend to plant or machinery.

A change of use will not involve any physical change in the land. Whether or not a change is considered 'material' depends largely on a subjective judgment and is mainly, in the legal jargon, 'a matter of fact and degree'. Generally speaking, this will be where the new use is substantially different from the existing use, or where there has been an intensification of an existing use of such a scale that its character has changed significantly.

Section 55 of the 1990 Act excludes certain operations and uses from the definition. These include:

- maintenance, improvement or alteration works to a building which are either internal or do not 'materially affect' the external appearance

- the use of any buildings or other land within the curtilage of a dwellinghouse for any purpose incidental to the enjoyment of the dwellinghouse
- the use of any land, or buildings on that land, for the purposes of agriculture or forestry.

In addition, various minor matters, classes of development and certain changes of use are exempted from the general need for permission, either because they are deemed not to be development for the purposes of planning control or because permission is automatically granted by a development order or other instrument.

Permitted development

So-called 'permitted development' rights are set out in the Town and Country Planning (General Permitted Development) Order 1995 (GPDO), as amended, and these are explained in *DoE Circular 9/95: General Development Order Consolidation*. The effect of the GPDO is to permit, in certain circumstances, a wide range of carefully defined, relatively small-scale and normally uncontentious developments, including, for example, small house extensions and alterations, porches, garden sheds, hard surfaces, swimming pools and means of enclosure. In England, Part 1, Schedule 2 of the GPDO, which grants permission for certain types of householder development, was amended significantly with effect from 1 October 2008. There are now, therefore, important differences between England and Wales. The Planning Portal includes an interactive visual guide for householders. For one planning officer's detailed examination of the GPDO, and the difficulties in interpreting its provisions, see www.planningjungle.com.

The GPDO also permits certain changes of use, temporary buildings and uses, caravan sites, agricultural buildings and operations, industrial and warehouse development, and other minor operations. At Appendix B we have listed the main categories of permitted development.

In certain areas, permitted development rights are more restricted. For example, within a conservation area, a World Heritage Site, a National Park, an Area of Outstanding Natural Beauty (AONB) or the Norfolk and Suffolk Broads, planning permission is required for certain types of development that would not otherwise require it. Moreover, local authorities are able to remove permitted development rights by issuing an 'article 4 direction', typically within a conservation area. Certain permitted development rights can also be withdrawn by conditions on a planning permission. In addition, permitted development rights may not apply where a proposed development is caught by regulations dealing with the conservation of natural habitats or environmental assessment.

In England, the government is proposing to widen the scope of permitted development rights so that many more minor extensions and alterations to non-domestic developments can be built without the need for express planning permission from the LPA.

The Town and Country (Use Classes) Order 1987, as amended, also provides that changes of use within broad classes are exempt from planning control. A number of changes to this order came into force in April 2005, and these are explained in *ODPM Circular 03/2005: Changes of Use of Buildings and Land*. A simple summary of the revised use classes can be found at Appendix C.

Local Development Orders and Simplified Planning Zones

The Planning and Compulsory Purchase Act 2004 ('the 2004 Act') enables planning authorities to extend permitted development rights by making a Local Development Order (LDO). In effect, an LDO grants permission for the type of development specified in the order, or for any class of development, thereby removing the need for the developer to apply to the planning authority. The LDO can relate to the whole of a planning authority's area, or just to part of it – such as to a specific site. Potentially, of course, such an order may stimulate development in areas requiring regeneration and help make the planning system quicker and more efficient. However, little interest has so far been shown by planning authorities in making LDOs, although, following research commissioned by the Planning Advisory Service and published on its website in March 2009, this could change.

In addition, Simplified Planning Zones exist in some parts of the country. These allow certain types of development to take place without specific planning permission, provided a number of conditions are met.

Assessing the need for permission

The whole issue of what constitutes development and requires permission is somewhat complicated and is subject to extensive qualifications and restrictions. Inevitably, there is scope for wide-ranging differences in interpretation, and clarification of certain aspects has therefore frequently fallen to the courts. In cases where the position is unclear, it is therefore prudent to discuss the matter with the local planning authority (LPA) and obtain an informal written opinion. A cautious approach is often the best course of action. Where it is thought that something under consideration might give rise to an objection, assume the worst; it is likely that the LPA will argue that permission is required. In appropriate circumstances, a formal application may also be made for a 'certificate of lawfulness' for the proposed development.

See also:
Certificates of
Lawfulness,
page 66

When considering the need for permission, it is important to investigate the planning history of the site. Practices at LPAs vary, so it is best to telephone to establish whether prior notice of any visit and personal search is required (some authorities may require up to 48 hours' notice). The better equipped LPAs are able to produce a computer print-out, detailing previous planning applications. Others may rely on a card index system or a plotting sheet. Details of recent planning applications should be published on the LPA's website. In many cases, it might be necessary to inspect historical application files themselves, and this is generally permissible under freedom of information legislation. Such files might be held on microfiche, CD-ROM, or in archive storage and these will need to be retrieved. Local authorities often charge for such a service and for providing copies of background papers. However, if there is a copy of the officer's report to committee on any history file, this will usually summarise relevant issues and short-cut the need for a full review of all the background papers.

Some planning permissions contain a condition withdrawing certain permitted development rights, thus expressly requiring permission for a particular development. The most common are conditions restricting various changes of use (typically those within use class Groups A and B, which relate to shops, financial services, food and drink, and business uses), or which prevent extensions and/ or the insertion of windows (especially in the case of small dwellings and barn conversions). Other conditions might have been imposed to provide that any permission applies only to a named person and therefore does not run with the land (this is known as a 'personal permission'). If such limitations have been revealed, it might be necessary to check whether these have been repeated in any planning agreements entered into with the council.

See also:
Planning
obligations,
developer
contributions
and 'planning
gain', page
107

Irrespective of whether planning permission is required, it might be necessary to obtain other special consents (the most common examples are explained later).

In addition, do not forget that Building Regulations approval will normally be required, but this is dealt with under separate legislation.

Who can apply?

Anyone can apply for planning permission on any land provided the application is accompanied by the relevant ownership certificate. This will confirm that the applicant is the owner, or that notice has been served on the owner (where the name and address is known to the applicant) or, in other cases, that certain steps have been taken to ascertain the name and address of any owner, including placing an advertisement in a local newspaper.

Who processes planning applications?

Most planning applications are processed by district or unitary authorities, or by the relevant National Park authority. The former include London borough councils, metropolitan and non-metropolitan councils and, in Wales, county or county borough councils. However, outside unitary authorities, certain applications (mainly involving minerals and waste disposal) are dealt with by county councils.

See also:
Administration
of the system,
page 11
In addition, there may be special arrangements for dealing with applications in certain regeneration or growth areas, as discussed earlier under Section 1. However, these account for only a handful of authorities.

In certain circumstances, the Secretary of State (or the National Assembly for Wales) may intervene and 'call in' an application for decision, although this happens in only a few, generally high-profile, cases involving issues of national or regional importance. The most common examples relate to controversial developments in the Green Belt, wind farms, major housing schemes on greenfield sites, certain proposals affecting listed buildings and large out-of-centre shopping schemes. In England, the criteria for calling in an application are set out in a ministerial policy statement made on 16 June 1999, as included at Annexe B of the Procedural Guidance published by the Planning Inspectorate in April 2009: *Planning Appeals and Called-in Planning Applications* (PINS 01/2009). Following the Greater London Act 2007, the Mayor of London is also empowered to call in and determine strategically important planning applications, as well as to direct that proposals that conflict with the London Plan be refused.

Applications are assessed by planning officers, most of whom are members of the Royal Town Planning Institute (RTPI) and so are chartered town planners. Some planning officers may be chartered surveyors (planning and development division), while others may also be architects or hold qualifications in urban design. The person who is allocated a particular application is usually referred to as the 'case officer'.

Planning officers may determine certain types of application themselves, especially for non-contentious householder or other minor developments, under so-called 'delegated powers' (these are clearly defined executive powers given by the councillors to their officers). More complex or controversial applications, such as those involving major developments, significant policy issues, listed buildings or objections from third parties, are usually decided by a committee of elected members (normally known as the planning and/or development committee, board or panel). Most local authorities operate a protocol whereby members can intervene and call in an application that might be listed for a decision by officers under delegated powers, so that the relevant committee can consider and determine the application itself.

Main types of application

As architects, the main types of planning application that you are likely to come across relate to:

- outline permission
- reserved matters approval
- full permission
- retrospective permission for the retention of development already carried out
- removal or variation of conditions attached to a permission.

Other applications, stemming mainly from special controls, might also be encountered, including those for:

- listed building consent
- conservation area consent
- advertisement regulations consent
- Tree Preservation Order consent
- hedgerow regulations consent
- Certificates of Lawfulness ('lawful development certificates').

Outline permission

The main purpose of an outline application is to determine whether the general principle of a proposed development is acceptable, especially where a major development proposal is envisaged. It is, however, possible at this stage to seek specific approval of a detailed planning matter, or for this to be reserved as a matter for subsequent approval. Following changes implemented in 2006, the 'reserved matters' (previously comprising the siting, design, external appearance, means of access and the landscaping of the site) are now defined as:

- *layout* – the way in which buildings, routes and open spaces are provided within the development and their relationship to buildings and spaces outside the development
- *scale* – the height, width and length of each building proposed in relation to its surroundings
- *appearance* – the aspects of a building or place which determine the visual impression it makes, excluding the external built form of the development
- *access* – this covers accessibility to and within the site for vehicles, cycles and pedestrians in terms of the positioning and treatment of access and circulation routes and how these fit into the surrounding access network, and
- *landscaping* – this is the treatment of private and public space to enhance or protect the site's amenity through hard and soft measures, for example, through planting of trees or hedges or screening by fences or walls.

As part of the changes to the planning application system introduced in 2006, the government has done away with the practice of 'red-lining' outline applications that have little supporting detail. An outline application must now include a basic level of information on the proposed use and amount of development, an indicative site layout and scale parameters, and indicative access points. A Design and Access Statement (DAS) is also required at this stage. We say more about the information necessary to support an outline application later, under the heading *Preparing the application* (page 74).

Because of the more onerous information requirements for outline applications, in our experience many applicants consider that they might just as well seek full permission in the first instance. But there will, of course, still be circumstances where an outline application would be more appropriate.

Acceptability of outline permissions, their renewal and conditions

Outline applications are not normally acceptable in sensitive locations, such as conservation areas, the settings of listed buildings or in Green Belts. Neither can they be used for changes of use.

Outline permissions are granted subject to various conditions, including those specifying time limits and requiring the subsequent approval of reserved matters. The 2004 Act removed the previous overall time limit of five years. But applications for the approval of reserved matters must still be made within three years and the development begun within two years from their final approval. These 'default periods' are deemed to apply even if not stated on the 'notice of permission', although LPAs are able to specify longer or shorter time limits in appropriate circumstances and may subsequently extend these following an application to renew the permission.

See also: Renewing existing permissions, page 63

It should be noted that, when seeking to renew an outline permission before its expiry, the courts have held that local authorities are entitled to reconsider the principle of the proposed development. They are also able to impose new conditions, not previously attached to the original permission.

The general principle is that conditions should be applied at the outline stage in the process, and that the only conditions that can be imposed when the reserved matters are approved are conditions that directly relate to those matters.

Reserved matters approval

The details of reserved matters may be submitted for approval separately or together, or for different parts of the site. A reserved matters application must be made within the time limits and come within the scope of the outline permission; it is therefore not possible, for example, to materially increase the size of the site or depart substantially from the terms.

Relevant legislation does not require an application for the approval of reserved matters to be accompanied by a DAS, since this will have been submitted at the outline stage. However, some LPAs may ask for a statement updating the contents of the DAS and explaining how its design principles have been followed through when working up the details of the permitted scheme. When considering applications for the approval of the reserved matters, planning authorities are restricted to considering the relevant details and may not revisit the principle of the development or apply any condition that could have been reasonably foreseen at the outline stage. A good example of an acceptable condition imposed on a reserved matters approval is one that seeks to withdraw certain permitted development rights, while the imposition of an agricultural occupancy restriction, for example, would not be appropriate at the reserved matters stage. Neither is it necessary to repeat any condition on an approval of reserved matters that has been attached to the outline permission.

Full permission

An application for full permission requires detailed drawings to illustrate the proposed development. Clearly, both the principle of the development and the submitted details will be considered by the planning authority and further information or amendments may be sought as necessary. Where there is an existing outline permission, there is usually no merit in applying for full permission instead of seeking the approval of reserved matters, unless the proposed development fails to fall within the terms of the original permission.

Such applications are generally required in the case of proposed development within conservation areas and the setting of listed buildings, and often for certain proposals in sensitive areas where their visual impact needs to be assessed. In addition, full permission is required for householder developments, such as garages and extensions, and for changes of use and conversions, unless of course these are classed as permitted development.

The 2004 Act has reduced the 'default' lifespan of a full planning permission from five years to three years. The planning permission will lapse if development is not commenced within this period. However, planning authorities are able to increase or reduce the lifespan of a permission in appropriate circumstances, such as granting permission for a temporary period only, particularly in the case of certain changes of use where a trial run may be considered desirable in order to assess long-term impacts. Moreover, the government has indicated that the five-year default lifespan will be reinstated.

Retrospective applications

Where development has been carried out without the necessary permission, or in contravention of a condition of any permission (including those limiting the duration of a permission), section 73A of the 1990 Act makes it possible to 'regularise' such unauthorised development by way of a retrospective application to the LPA, and this will be assessed in the normal way. An application to retain an unauthorised development must therefore be considered impartially and on its own merits. The applicant should not be allowed to benefit from, or conversely be disadvantaged by, jumping the gun or departing from the terms of an existing permission.

Renewing existing permissions

The practice of extending the time limit for the implementation of an existing permission before it has expired by varying the relevant condition was abolished from August 2006. However, in response to concerns expressed by the development industry and local planning authorities, in England the government has recently introduced a new simplified procedure that has a similar effect, although the successful outcome of such an application is in fact a replacement planning permission with a new time limit.

As a general rule, applications to renew an existing permission should be refused only where:

- there has been some material change in planning circumstances since the original permission was granted (for example, a change in some relevant planning policy for the area, changes to relevant highway considerations, or the publication by the government of new planning policy guidance material to the renewal application)
- there is continued failure to begin the development, which contributes to uncertainty about the future pattern of development in the area
- the application is premature because the permission still has a reasonable time to run.

Removal or variation of conditions

Application may also be made under section 73 of the 1990 Act to develop land without complying with certain conditions attached to a previous permission. In effect, this allows for the variation or removal of planning conditions. In order to do this, the permission must still be alive; otherwise a fresh application is required. In assessing such an application, the local authority is required to consider only the conditions subject to which planning permission should be granted and, irrespective of the outcome, the original permission remains unaltered.

Because a section 73 application is an application for a new permission, which leaves the existing permission untouched, it must be accompanied by a DAS (where one is required). Applications under section 73 may no longer be made by letter only but should be made using the national 1APP application form (see later under *Preparing the application: Forms*, page 74).

Listed building and conservation area consent

As explained in Section 3, 'listed building consent' is required for works involving the demolition of all or part of a listed building and for both external and internal alterations and/or extensions that would affect its character. In many instances, these works will involve development requiring planning permission. Thus an application for listed building consent will often duplicate a planning application and will normally be submitted at the same time to enable development and conservation issues to be considered together.

'Conservation area consent' is required in certain circumstances, such as where the demolition of a non-listed building within a conservation area is proposed.

No fee is payable to the LPA for applications for listed building or conservation area consent, and they are processed in essentially the same way as planning applications.

Further information is set out in the Planning (Listed Buildings and Conservation Areas) Regulations 1990, and in *Planning Policy Guidance 15: Planning and the Historic Environment* (PPG15), issued in 1994, as amended by Circulars 01/2001 and 09/2005, which discuss arrangements for handling heritage applications, and CLG Circular 01/2007, which contains revised principles for use in listing decisions and replaces paragraphs 6.1 to 6.40 of PPG15. In Wales, reference should be made to *WO Circular 61/96: Planning and the Historic Environment: Historic buildings and conservation areas*.

See also:
Listed
buildings,
page 35

Advertisement regulations consent

The control of advertisements forms part of the planning system and is quite complex, especially with regard to those advertisements that are excluded from control and those falling within specified classes that benefit from deemed consent. These do not require the express consent of the planning authority, provided certain conditions are met. Because of the difficulties of applying the relevant regulations (the Town and Country Planning (Control of Advertisements) (England) Regulations 2007 and the Town and Country Planning (Control of Advertisements) Regulations 1992 for Wales), many planning authorities have a particular officer to deal with advertisement applications. Similarly, the Planning Inspectorate has a specialist team of inspectors to handle any subsequent appeals.

Unless you are satisfied that the need for consent is clear, it would be prudent to discuss this with the local authority. Generally, consent is required for the following:

- most illuminated signs
- nearly all poster hoardings
- fascia signs and projecting signs on shopfronts or business premises where the top edge of the sign is more than 4.6 metres above ground level
- most advertisements on gable-ends.

The procedure for applying for advertisement regulations consent is more or less the same as that for a planning application. The LPA's consideration of its merits is restricted to two issues:

- amenity
- public safety.

Should consent be refused, there is a right of appeal to the Planning Inspectorate, on behalf of the Secretary of State.

Because of the considerable complexity of the advertisement control regime, some planning consultants specialise in this area of work. You would therefore be well advised to seek their services, should you become involved in such matters.

In England, further advice is set out in *Planning Policy Guidance 19: Outdoor Advertisement Control* (PPG19, March 1992) and *CLG Circular 03/2007: Town and Country Planning (Control of Advertisements) (England) Regulations 2007*. In Wales, where the Town and Country Planning (Control of Advertisements) Regulations 1992 apply, see *Technical Advice Note 7: Outdoor Advertisement Control* (TAN7, 1996). In addition, an explanatory booklet entitled *Outdoor Advertisements and Signs – A guide for advertisers* can be downloaded from the CLG website.

Certificates of Lawfulness

Sections 191 and 192 of the 1990 Act provide that anyone (not just a person with a legal interest in the land) may apply to the LPA for a Certificate of Lawfulness, more commonly known as a 'lawful development certificate' (LDC). Such a certificate is a legal document that confirms that the following is lawful:

- an *existing* operation on, or use of land, or some activity being carried out in breach of a planning condition, or
- a *proposed* operation on or use of land.

The former is referred to as a 'certificate of lawfulness of existing use or development' (CLEUD) while the latter is known as a 'certificate of lawfulness of proposed use or development' (CLOPUD).

Annex 8 of *DoE Circular 10/97: Enforcing Planning Control: Legislative provisions and procedural requirements* explained that development or other activity on land is lawful for planning purposes if it falls within one of the following categories and is not in breach of a planning condition or limitation:

- It does not fall within the definition of development.
- It is specifically excluded from the definition of development (such as the use of land for agriculture).
- It falls within the definition of development but is exempted from the need to apply for permission.
- It benefits from an existing planning permission.
- It is permitted development.
- It benefits from deemed planning permission by virtue of compliance with the requirements of an effective enforcement notice.
- It took place before 1 July 1948.
- It is development by or on behalf of the Crown (note: under the 2004 Act, the Crown's immunity from the normal planning process ceased on 7 June 2006).
- The time for taking enforcement action has expired.

"the time limits for taking enforcement action are four years in the case of operational development and for any change of use to a single dwellinghouse, and ten years for all other changes of use"

As far as the last point is concerned, the time limits for taking enforcement action are four years in the case of operational development and for any change of use to a single dwellinghouse, and ten years for all other changes of use.

The effect of the grant of a CLEUD is to make the specified development immune from enforcement action, provided that it is not already in breach of an existing enforcement notice. Essentially, a CLEUD is equivalent to the grant of permission. It will be precisely defined by the planning authority, with specific reference to the area of land to which the certificate relates, and will be conclusive.

Applications for CLEUDs are considered solely on the weight of the supporting documentary evidence, applying the test of 'the balance of probability'. Basically, this means that it is more likely than not that the claim is true, and is less strict than the criminal test of 'beyond reasonable doubt'. The planning merits of the development are therefore not relevant to the LPA's consideration. As the onus of proof is firmly on the applicant and only legal issues are involved, solicitors often handle such applications, or at least have a hand in the preparation of evidence. That evidence might include, for example:

- affidavits
- statutory declarations
- accounts
- rating records
- receipts
- vehicle registration documents
- utilities bills.

As the planning authority is not able to impose any conditions when granting an LDC, a CLEUD is likely to be of greater benefit to an applicant than the possible alternative of retrospective permission. However, the planning authority is able to issue a certificate of a different description from that applied for, in order to define precisely and unambiguously what has been substantiated by the submitted evidence.

The effect of a CLOPUD is not the equivalent of a grant of permission for a proposed development. Rather, unless there has been some material change in circumstances since the application date specified in the certificate, it would be lawful to proceed with the proposed development. Such a change might include, for example, the curtailment of permitted development rights through an article 4 direction or the designation of a conservation area.

There is a right of appeal to the Planning Inspectorate (on behalf of the Secretary of State) against a planning authority's refusal to grant an LDC.

Trees and hedgerows

Trees and hedgerows can be protected in several ways and thus consent may be required for their felling, lopping or for other surgical works.

Section 198 of the 1990 Act enables local authorities to make a Tree Preservation Order (TPO) in respect of individual trees, groups of trees or areas of woodland, where this is expedient in the interests of amenity. TPOs must be made in accordance with the procedures set out in the Town and Country Planning (Trees) Regulations 1999 and, although objections may be lodged to proposed TPOs, there is no right of appeal against their subsequent confirmation by the local authority. However, in certain circumstances it may be possible to challenge the TPO in the High Court on a point of law. Otherwise, appeals may be made only where a local authority has subsequently refused to grant TPO consent.

The effect of a TPO is to require the consent of the local authority for the 'cutting down, topping, lopping, uprooting, wilful damage, or wilful destruction' of any tree which is the subject of such a TPO. In addition, in certain circumstances landowners are placed under a duty to replace protected trees that have been removed. TPO provisions do not apply to trees that are dying or dead, or have become dangerous, where it may be necessary for the prevention or abatement of a nuisance, or where exemptions are conferred by other relevant legislation.

Where works to a protected tree are required for the purposes of carrying out authorised development, the provisions of the TPO no longer apply. Thus a planning permission will override such protection.

As part of the government's planning reform programme, the Town and Country Planning (Determination of Appeals by Appointed Persons) (Prescribed Classes) (Amendment) (England) Regulations 2008, which came into force on 6 April 2008, and the Town and Country Planning (Trees) (Amendment) (England) Regulations 2008, which came into force on 1 October 2008, introduced the following changes in England:

- a mandatory standard application form, with requirements for supporting information, which must be used when applying for consent to carry out work to trees protected by a TPO

- a fast-track appeal process for cases where LPAs refuse consent, impose conditions, issue an article 5 certificate or a tree replacement notice, and
- the power for the Planning Inspectorate to process these appeals and empower planning inspectors, rather than the Secretary of State, to make decisions on them.

Further information on tree preservation may be found in the Town and Country Planning (Trees) Regulations 1999 (England and Wales), as amended in 2008 for England only, and in *Tree Preservation Orders: A guide to the law and good practice* (April 2000, with an addendum published in May 2009 that explains recent changes in England) and *Protected Trees – A guide to tree preservation procedures* (October 2008). Both guides are published on the CLG website. In Wales, reference should be made to *Technical Advice Note 10: Tree Preservation Orders* (TAN10, 1997).

Trees within a designated conservation area enjoy a similar level of protection to those subject to a TPO, subject to certain exceptions and procedural differences. These include a general requirement to give the LPA six weeks' notice of any intention to fell, lop, top or otherwise damage a tree. The authority may either consent to the proposed works or make a TPO. If it does neither within this period, then this can be used in defence of the carrying out of such works, provided that these are done within two years. Trees under a prescribed size, some species and certain acts may be exempted under the relevant regulations. It should be noted that more onerous replanting obligations apply than under the TPO regime.

When granting planning permission, local authorities will frequently seek to retain or protect important trees by imposing appropriate conditions. However, government advice is that the long-term protection of trees should be secured by TPOs rather than by conditions.

Under the Hedgerows Regulations 1997, it is unlawful to remove or destroy countryside hedges that are at least 20 metres in length, over 30 years old and contain certain species of plant without first obtaining the permission of the local authority. Any hedgerow within the curtilage of a dwelling is excluded. Where permission is required, the LPA will assess the importance of the hedgerow using criteria set out in the regulations. The leaflet *The Hedgerows Regulations: Your question answered* provides a brief summary of the law, while more detailed guidance is given in *The Hedgerows Regulations 1997: A guide to the law and good practice* (both produced by Defra). See also the Hedgelink website: www.hedgelink.org.uk, which has been set up by the Steering Group for the delivery of the UK Biodiversity Action Plan for hedgerows as the first source of information on hedgerows.

Preparing and submitting planning applications

It is perhaps self-evident that the key to a successful planning application will often lie in its careful preparation and presentation. However, all too frequently applications are not validated because they are inadequate. Their processing may subsequently be delayed, or they may ultimately be refused, because of some failure to take into account a matter that should have been reasonably clear at the outset.

In *Keeping Out of Trouble* (2006), Owen Luder points out that most clients are not fully aware of the potential problems and delays with obtaining planning approvals. When dealing with town planning applications he advises:

> Never be anything other that totally realistic about the time required for obtaining the necessary planning approval and the lack of certainty in obtaining an acceptable planning approval.

He also gives sound advice on keeping clients fully up to speed with the progress of their applications and the tactics to follow when strong local opposition is foreseen.

Some applicants underestimate the sheer complexity of the planning process and look upon it as something of an unwelcome formality. Recognising that this is not the case, and embracing it as a 'development partner', will help greatly in ensuring that potential problems are anticipated and that emerging projects succeed. In addition, the increasing need for specialist advice of one sort or another – to address the diverse issues that are often thrown up – should always be borne in mind.

"Perfect preparation and partnership prevents poor performance in planning!"

The reforms to the planning system have placed great emphasis on early consultation and 'front-loading', with greatly increased requirements and expectations. So it is vital that your proposals are prepared with the utmost care. To adapt a well-known military truism: perfect preparation and partnership prevents poor performance in planning!

Pre-application discussions

Before submitting a planning application, particularly for complex or larger developments, you should discuss the proposal with an officer of the LPA. Government advice – as set out in *Planning Policy Statement 1: Delivering Sustainable Development* (PPS1) – is that pre-application discussions are critically important and benefit both developers and LPAs in ensuring a better mutual understanding of objectives and the constraints that exist. Both planning authorities and applicants are therefore exhorted to take a positive attitude towards early engagement in pre-application discussions so that formal applications can be dealt with in a more certain and speedy manner, and the quality of decisions can be better assured.

In recent years, limited resources and the pressure to meet performance targets have meant that many authorities have been unable to engage fully in such pre-application discussions, and sometimes not at all. Nevertheless, the increasing importance and value of pre-application discussions was recognised in the final report of the Barker Review of Land Use Planning (December 2006), and is now the subject of a practical guide produced by the Planning Advisory Service (PAS) in collaboration with CLG, representatives of the development industry and the planning profession, whose advice you should follow. *Constructive Talk: Investing in pre-application discussions* (May 2007) is available on the PAS website.

Changes to local government legislation mean that authorities are now able to charge for pre-application advice, although most currently do not. Where charges are made, these are usually on a sliding scale according to the size and complexity of the proposed development. Irrespective of whether a payment is required, many councils have introduced their own special procedures and requirements for such pre-application discussions or guidance. You will therefore need to check these. But do be aware that with some authorities, pre-application discussions may involve lengthy delays or require the submission of a significant amount of detail. In such cases, it may be more productive or cost-effective to submit an early application as a 'tester', consider the planning authority's response and, if faced with a refusal, then withdraw the application and submit a revised proposal as a 'free go' (where no new fee would be payable).

During pre-application discussions, you should seek clarification of the issues and planning policies that are likely to have to be addressed, the information that will need to be submitted with the application (including any impact statements or specialist reports) and the application's chances of success. Try to get the planning authority's informal opinions confirmed in writing. This will help to avoid unnecessary delays in processing the application and ensure that possible pitfalls are identified early on. It will also provide a record of such discussions in the event that someone else subsequently deals with the application.

While it is wise to seek such advice, it should be understood that it is given in good faith, without prejudice to the formal consideration of any planning application by the local authority. Try to speak to the planning officer who is familiar with the area and would eventually consider the application, when submitted. If you can, or if it is particularly important – for example, where it is necessary to inspect inaccessible buildings or for judgments to be made on matters of 'visual amenity' – arrange to meet on site.

Do your homework!

Pre-application approaches to the planning authority are likely to be more productive if some basic preparation is undertaken beforehand, not least because it will mean that you are already aware of relevant issues and will have a much better idea of those that could require particular attention. You will also know which questions you should ask, and have time to consider how you might best respond to the questions that are likely to be put to you. This is particularly the case if the proposal is likely to be controversial. If possible, therefore, you should always try to undertake the following:

- Investigate the planning history of the site and consider anything that might be relevant to the proposal.
- Check adopted and/or emerging designation of the site under any Local Plan, Unitary Development Plan (UDP) or Development Plan Documents (DPDs), and any policies relevant to the proposal (see our suggested checklist at Appendix D).
- In the case of larger sites, check whether a 'planning brief' has been prepared.
- Familiarise yourself with the relevant development control/management and highway standards adopted by the council. These will normally be set out in a Local Plan, UDP, DPD, in a locally adopted design guide or in other supplementary planning guidance and SPDs. The most common standards relate to access, roads and parking, public and private amenity space provision, maintenance of residential amenity (e.g. overlooking and overshadowing) and to affordable housing provision. Check the threshold above which affordable

housing provisions kick in, together with any requirements for developer contributions towards infrastructure, community facilities and so forth. These could have a significant bearing on the viability of the proposed development.

- Although it may appear blindingly obvious, make sure that you look at the site (alarmingly, we are aware of cases where agents have relied on photographs!). Assess for yourself the site's characteristics, its constraints and opportunities, and its setting and general surroundings. If necessary, arrange for a preliminary survey, to include the location and condition of any trees on site and any changes of level. The information you collect should form part of a drawn site appraisal or setting analysis.

- Prepare a simple preliminary sketch to show the form of the proposed development and send this to the relevant planning officer, in advance of the meeting. This will enable them to consider its merits informally and, if necessary, seek the views of more senior officers and colleagues in other departments. It may also be appropriate to prepare other material, such as a draft DAS, the heads of terms for a section 106 agreement or an artist's impression of the development.

- Check whether the planning authority has published its own planning guidance on its website. This may explain its particular requirements, the structure of the planning department and the council's decision-making procedures, and set out other useful information.

- For larger, more complex proposals, consider whether a formal Environmental Impact Assessment is either mandatory or could be deemed necessary. This is often overlooked, sometimes resulting in a permission that is open to judicial review from objectors.

- Find out how long it is likely to take for any application to be processed, the dates of relevant planning committee meetings and the extent of any delegated powers. For large-scale proposals, check whether a Planning Performance Agreement would be appropriate (for information on these agreements, see the guidance on the ATLAS pages of the PAS website and check out the ATLAS website itself at www.atlasplanning.com).

- Always allow sufficient time to obtain permission before development is due to start, and do not simply assume that your application is one that can be determined quickly or that permission will be automatically granted.

See also: What happens to your application and what should you do? page 93

Where a controversial development is proposed, it is crucial to secure grass-roots or other third party support. It is therefore important to involve the local community and others at the outset and to carry out some form of informal consultation exercise. This might include discussing your ideas with the parish or community council, local councillors, residents' groups or others who are likely to be formally consulted on the application. If the proposed development involves a new or altered access, new roads or traffic generation issues, you should discuss the matter informally with the highway authority as many proposals that are otherwise acceptable in planning terms fail on highways grounds. Similarly, if the proposal includes works to a listed building or there are protected trees on site and so forth, separate discussions with the council's conservation officer or landscape division might also be helpful.

Preparing the application

Forms

Other than in the case of mineral developments, all applications to LPAs in England and Wales must be made on the new national standard application form (1APP). Previously, application forms varied widely across the country, causing confusion and inconsistencies in the information that each authority required to be submitted. So, in line with its commitment to streamline and simplify the planning application process, 1APP has now standardised requirements. The form may be accessed either directly through the Planning Portal or via a local authority's own website. Different versions of the form are available, depending on whether an outline or full permission is sought or some other consent or approval. Each form requires different levels of information and supporting documentation to be submitted.

Regardless of which particular version of 1APP must be completed, it is important to answer the questions comprehensively and to follow the relevant guidance notes. Think carefully about the description of the proposed development as any permission will relate specifically to this (and, in the case of new or listed buildings, there may be VAT implications). If necessary, describe the development more fully in the covering letter or in the DAS, if one is required. Make sure that the relevant ownership/agricultural holdings certificates have been completed (see below). And, of course, do not forget to keep a copy of the application form as this may be needed for any subsequent appeal.

A total of four copies of the application will need to be submitted to the planning authority (the original plus three copies). Applications may be submitted either electronically, via the Planning Portal, or in paper format. Although the govern-ment wishes to encourage applicants to submit applications electronically wher-ever possible, as it considers this provides opportunities for streamlining procedures and reducing costs, this has yet to take off fully. So far, only around 25 per cent of all applications are lodged online. In some instances, the electronic submission of an application may even be resisted by the local authority or deemed inappropriate because of the nature, size and complexity of the drawings and supporting information. In any event, do be aware of the local authority's specific requirements for following this procedure and the need normally to provide additional copies on CD or DVD.

Ownership/agricultural holdings certificates

A planning authority cannot entertain an application for planning permission unless the relevant certificates concerning the ownership of the application site have been completed. All applications, except for approval of reserved matters, discharge or variation of conditions, TPOs and express consent to display an advertisement, must therefore include the appropriate certificate of ownership, together with an agricultural holdings certificate (regardless of whether or not the site includes an agricultural holding). All agricultural tenants must be notified prior to the submission of the application.

For the purposes of the ownership certificate, an 'owner' is defined as anyone with a freehold interest, or a leasehold interest with an unexpired term of not less than seven years. Certificate A should be completed when the applicant is the sole owner; Certificate B, when the owner is known to the applicant; and Certificate C or D when not all or none of the owners of the site are known, respectively. Any owners other than the applicant must be served notice of the application.

Application fees

Unless exempt, all applications must be accompanied by the correct application fee, which is payable to the planning authority and, except in certain circum-stances, is non-refundable. For both England and Wales, the relevant fees are set out in the Town and Country Planning (Fees for Applications and Deemed Applications) Regulations 1989, as amended. In England, the fees are explained in CLG Circular 04/2008. Among other things, the circular gives advice on how fees should be calculated, exemptions and concessions, and what to do if the amount that should be paid is disputed.

If an authority refuses to validate, register and determine an application because it considers that the correct fee has not been paid, the applicant may, after eight weeks (or 13 weeks for major applications) appeal to the Planning Inspectorate on the grounds of the application's non-determination (though only if the application is, in all other respects, capable of validation). In those circumstances, the Inspectorate, on behalf of the Secretary of State, must then consider whether it has jurisdiction in the case, whether the application is otherwise valid, and whether the amount paid in by the applicant was correct.

The fees regulations provide that where an application is withdrawn or refused, where an appeal or a 'called-in' application has been rejected by the Secretary of State, or where the applicant has appealed to the Secretary of State on the grounds of non-determination of their application, the same applicant may submit one further application for the same character or description of development on the same site, or part of that site, as a 'free go'. However, in order to qualify for this exemption, the resubmission must be made within 12 months of the date when the previous application was refused or, in the case of a withdrawn application, within 12 months from when the application was submitted.

The existence of the free go has taken on increased importance in recent years as planning authorities have become more reluctant to negotiate and allow

See also:
Negotiations
and tactics,
page 101
changes to an application after its submission, for fear that by so doing they would fail to determine it within the statutory time limits and miss their performance targets. We say more about negotiations and tactics later.

Design and Access Statements

Since 10 August 2006 (in England) and 1 June 2009 (in Wales), it has been a statutory requirement that applications for both outline and full planning permission be accompanied by a DAS, unless the application relates to one of the following:

• a material change of use of land and buildings (unless it also involves operational development)

- engineering or mining operations
- householder developments (except where any part of a dwellinghouse or its curtilage falls within a National Park, Site of Special Scientific Interest, conservation area, AONB, World Heritage Site or The Broads).

A DAS is a report accompanying and supporting a planning application that should seek to explain and justify the proposal in a structured way. The level of detail required in a DAS will depend on the scale and complexity of the application, and the length of the statement will vary accordingly. In England, the precise requirements for a DAS are set out in article 4C of the Town and Country Planning (General Development Procedure) Order 1995 (GDPO) and in *CLG Circular 01/2006: Guidance on Changes to the Development Control System*. In short, these require that a DAS must explain the design principles and concepts that have been applied to the amount, layout, scale, landscaping and appearance of the development. In addition, the DAS must:

- demonstrate the steps taken to appraise the physical, social, economic and policy context of the development and how the design of the development takes that context into account in relation to its proposed use and each of the aspects specified above
- explain the policy adopted as to access, and how policies relating to access in relevant Local Development Documents have been taken into account
- state what, if any, consultation has been undertaken on issues relating to access to the development and what account has been taken of the outcome of any such consultation
- explain how any specific issues that might affect access to the development have been addressed, how prospective users will be able to gain access to the development from the existing transport network, why the points of access to the site and the layout of access routes within the site have been chosen, and how features that ensure access to the development will be maintained.

Applications for listed building consent must also be accompanied by a DAS, which should address:

- the special architectural or historic interest of the building
- the particular physical features of the building that justify its designation as a listed building, and
- the building's setting.

While a DAS need not be very long, it is important to ensure that it covers the matters set out in the legislation. However, in our experience of reading DASs, it is clear that many statements fail to explain in plain and simple language the 'story' of a proposed development. Like Planning Supporting Statements (and there is no reason why these should not be combined with a DAS) the DAS will not only be read by officers dealing with or commenting on the application, but will also be studied by local residents and others who may be unfamiliar with the planning system. In addition, it will be taken into account by an inspector in the event of an appeal becoming necessary. Therefore, the DAS provides a valuable opportunity to sell your scheme and explain to those who may have difficulty in understanding complex drawings and technical reports how the proposed development ticks all the relevant boxes and so should be approved. Disappointingly, too many DASs fail to justify the proposed development properly in relation to relevant planning policies and standards and rely instead on a mere description of its main components. Given the primacy of the development plan, it is important that practitioners address these issues properly. Moreover, since the Planning Act 2008 requires persons or bodies exercising functions in relation to development plans to have regard to the desirability of achieving good design, the role of design in the planning process has been strengthened. It is vital that sufficient attention is given to producing a design that meets the planning authority's stated requirements.

In Wales, the contents of a DAS differ slightly and are set out at article 4D of the GDPO. Related WAG guidance is set out in Appendix 1 of *Technical Advice Note 12: Design* (TAN12), which was revised in 2009.

In England, the CABE best practice guide *Design and Access Statements – How to write, read and use them* (2006) supplements the advice in CLG Circular 01/2006. However, you should note that the government is proposing to simplify the requirements for all DASs by requiring a more straightforward explanation of how the context of the development influences its design, and to reduce the range of applications that require a DAS. Revised guidance on this subject is therefore expected.

Best practice on the validation of planning applications

In order to further speed up the registration and processing of planning applications, in December 2007 CLG issued *The Validation of Planning Applications: Guidance for local planning authorities*. This explains new procedures for the validation of planning applications by LPAs and itemises the drawings, sup-porting statements and other information that are likely to be required to support your application. The document replaces *Best Practice Guidance on the Validation of Planning Applications* (published by ODPM in March 2005). It intro-duces a 'national list' of compulsory requirements for all applications, and advises that LPAs should also consult on and adopt their own local lists. These local lists should set out any additional information that could be required to validate an application, which should be taken from the national list of recommended items included in the guidance. Planning authorities also have discretion to include other locally specific requirements, provided these can be justified.

However, in response to recommendations made in the Killian Pretty Review, in July 2009 the government published a consultation paper in which it proposes a number of changes to the policy and guidance on information requirements and the validation of planning applications. These can be summarised as follows:

* withdrawal of the current 'recommended national local list'
* introduction of a new, criteria-based, national policy requirement for LPAs preparing local lists to ensure they only ask for information that is relevant, necessary, proportionate and justified by national or local policy
* a requirement for LPAs to update their 'local list of information requirements' where necessary, having regard to this new policy requirement, by the end of December 2010
* refinement and improvement of the guidance on national list items, to encour-age a more proportionate approach and to clarify validation requirements
* a consideration of options for the external scrutiny of local lists, and
* encouragement of better submissions from applicants by proposing that applications for major development should be accompanied by a concise summary document.

Meanwhile, if you do not include the information required by the LPA's validation checklist with your application for planning permission, the authority would be entitled to declare the application invalid and not to register or process it. Nevertheless, CLG Circular 02/2008, which provides guidance on the use of the new 1APP form and the information that must be provided in order to validate a planning application in England, makes it clear that concerns over whether supporting information is of inadequate quality are not grounds for invalidating applications. Once an application has been validated, however, the planning authority retains the right under regulation 4 of the Town and Country Planning (Applications) Regulations 1988 to direct the applicant to provide any further information it deems necessary to help it consider an application (except for outline applications, for which further information can be requested but not further plans and drawings).

Before we discuss in some detail both compulsory and discretionary additional requirements (largely adapted from CLG Circular 02/2008), we remind you that all drawings must be drawn to a metric scale. It is also now common practice to add scale bars. Some authorities may insist that certain disclaimers, such as 'do not scale', are removed from drawings on the grounds that these could undermine any later enforcement action that might become necessary. You will therefore need to check the LPA's requirements.

Compulsory requirements for outline applications

CLG Circular 01/2006 sets out the scope of information to be submitted with an outline application. Even if layout, scale and access are to be reserved matters, as a minimum the following information is required:

- *Use* – the use or uses proposed for the development and any distinct development zones within the site identified.
- *Amount of development* – the amount of development proposed for each use.
- *Indicative layout* – an indicative layout with separate development zones proposed within the site boundary where appropriate.
- *Scale parameters* – an indication of the upper and lower limits for height, width and length of each building within the site boundary.
- *Indicative access points* – an area or areas in which the access point or points to the site will be situated.

In addition, outline applications must be accompanied by the correct fee, ownership/agricultural holdings certificate and a DAS explaining how the proposed development addresses relevant planning policies and responds to the site's constraints and opportunities. The DAS will form a link between the outline permission and the subsequent consideration of reserved matters.

Notwithstanding these minimum requirements, an LPA can also require the submission of further information to support an outline application. The LPA can also insist that the application includes any of the reserved matters for which the applicant had not sought approval, provided it does so within one month of receipt of the application.

Compulsory requirements for applications for full planning permission

Applications for full planning permission must be accompanied by the following:

- The *standard application form, ownership/agricultural holdings certificate* and the *correct fee*, where a fee is required (see above).
- *A location plan* based on an up-to-date map at a scale of 1:1250 or 1:2500. Where possible, the plan should show at least two named roads and surrounding buildings, which should be numbered or named. The application site should be edged clearly with a red line and include all land necessary to carry out the proposed development – for example, land required for access to the site from a public highway, visibility splays, landscaping, car parking and open areas around buildings. A blue line should be drawn around any other land owned by the applicant, close to or adjoining the application site.
- *A site layout plan*, drawn at a scale of 1:500 or 1:200 and showing:
  - the direction of north
  - the proposed development in relation to the site boundaries and other existing buildings on the site, with written dimensions, including those to the boundaries
  - all the buildings, roads and footpaths on land adjoining the site, including access arrangements
  - all public rights of way crossing or adjoining the site
  - the position of all trees on the site, and those on adjacent land that could influence or be affected by the development
  - the extent and type of any hard surfacing, and
  - boundary treatment including walls or fencing where this is proposed.

Depending on the type of application, other necessary plans may include the following:

- *Block plan of the site* (e.g. at a scale of 1:100 or 1:200), showing any site boundaries, the type and height of boundary treatment (such as walls and fences) and the position of any building or structure on the other side of such boundaries.
- *Existing and proposed elevations* (e.g. at a scale of 1:50 or 1:100), showing clearly the proposed works in relation to what is already there. All sides of

the proposal must be shown and these should indicate, where possible, the proposed building materials and the style, materials and finish of windows and doors. Blank elevations must also be included, if only to show that this is in fact the case. Where a proposed elevation adjoins another building or is in close proximity, the drawings should clearly show the relationship between the buildings and detail the positions of the openings on each property.

- *Existing and proposed floor plans* (e.g. at a scale of 1:50 or 1:100), explaining the proposal in detail. Where existing buildings or walls are to be demolished these should be clearly shown. The drawings should show details of the existing building(s) as well as those for the proposed development. New buildings should also be shown in context with adjacent buildings (including property numbers where applicable).

- *Existing and proposed site sections and finished floor and site levels* (e.g. at a scale of 1:50 or 1:100). Such plans should show a cross-section(s) through the proposed building(s). In all cases where a proposal involves a change in ground levels, illustrative drawings should be submitted to show both existing and finished levels, details of foundations and eaves, and how encroachment onto adjoining land is to be avoided. Full information should also be submitted to demonstrate how proposed buildings relate to existing site levels and neighbouring development. Such plans should show existing site levels and finished floor levels (with levels related to a fixed datum point off site) and also show the proposals in relation to adjoining buildings. This will be required for all applications involving new buildings. In the case of householder development, the levels may be evident from floor plans and elevations, but, particularly in the case of sloping sites, it will be necessary to show how proposals relate to existing ground levels or where ground levels outside the extension would be modified. Levels should also be taken into account in the formulation of design and access statements.

- *Roof plans* (e.g. at a scale of 1:50 or 1:100). A roof plan is used to show the shape of the roof and is typically drawn at a scale smaller than the scale used for the floor plans. Details such as the roofing material are typically specified on the roof plan.

Additional information that may be set out in local validation checklists

The following list sets out the range of additional information that the government has indicated could be required by LPAs before they validate an application (adapted from CLG Circular 02/2008). Since this will obviously vary according to the circumstances of each proposal, not all the information will be required in every case. Most of these reports will need to be prepared by other specialists. Where a number of different assessments are required, it may be appropriate to appoint a planning consultant or project manager to oversee and co-ordinate inputs.

- *Affordable housing statement.* Where development plan policies or Supplementary Planning Document (SPD) guidance require the provision of affordable housing, the LPA may insist on information on both the affordable housing and any open market housing, such as the number and mix of residential units, the numbers of habitable rooms and/or bedrooms, or the floor space of habitable areas of residential units, and plans of the units. If different levels of affordability or types of tenure are proposed for different units, this should be clearly and fully explained. The affordable housing statement should also include details of any Registered Social Landlords acting as partners in the development.
- *Air quality assessment.* A proposal for development within or adjacent to an air quality management area (AQMA), or which could itself result in the designation of an AQMA (or where the grant of permission would conflict with, or render unworkable, elements of an authority's air quality action plan), should be supported by such information as is necessary to allow a full consideration of its impact on the air quality of the area. Where AQMAs cover regeneration areas, developers should provide an air quality assessment as part of their planning application. Further advice is available in *PPS23: Planning and Pollution Control* (2004).
- *Biodiversity survey and report.* Where a proposed development could have impacts on wildlife and biodiversity, information should be provided on existing biodiversity interests and possible impacts on them to allow full consideration of those impacts. Where proposals are being made for mitigation and/or compensation measures, information to support those proposals will be needed. Where appropriate, accompanying plans should indicate any significant wildlife habitats or features and the location of habitats or any species protected under the Wildlife and Countryside Act 1981, the Conservation (Natural Habitats etc.) Regulations 1994 or the Protection of Badgers Act 1992. Applications for development in the countryside that will affect areas designated for their biodiversity interests are likely to need to include assessments of impacts and proposals for long-term maintenance and management.

This information might form part of an Environmental Statement (see below), where one is necessary. Certain proposals that include work such as the demolition of older buildings or roof spaces, removal of trees, scrub or hedgerows or alterations to water courses may affect protected species. Such proposals will need to provide information on the proposed works, including their potential impacts and any mitigation proposals for those impacts. See *PPS9: Biodiversity and Geological Conservation* (2005) and accompanying *ODPM Circular 06/2005: Biodiversity and Geological Conservation – Statutory obligations and their impact within the planning system,* and also *Planning for Biodiversity and Geological Conservation: A guide to good practice* (ODPM, 2006).

- *Daylight/sunlight assessment.* In circumstances where there is a potential adverse impact upon the current levels of sunlight/daylight enjoyed by adjoining properties or building(s), including associated gardens or amenity space, then applications may also need to be accompanied by a daylight/sunlight assessment. Further guidance is provided in BRE guidelines on daylight assessments, such as *Site Layout Planning for Daylight and Sunlight: A guide to good practice* (BRE Report 209, 1991).

- *Economic statement.* Applications may also need to be accompanied by a supporting statement of any regeneration benefits from the proposed development, including details of any new jobs that might be created or supported, the relative floor space totals for each proposed use (where known), any community benefits and reference to any regeneration strategies that might lie behind or be supported by the proposal.

- *Environmental Statement* (ES). Certain types of development that are likely to have significant effects on the environment because of their nature, size or location must be accompanied by a formal Environmental Impact Assessment (EIA), prepared in accordance with the Town and Country Planning (Environmental Impact Assessment) (England and Wales) Regulations 1999. Schedule 4 to the regulations sets out the information that should be included in an ES, which is the formal written statement of the findings of the EIA. The regulations require the developer to describe the likely significant effects of a development on the environment and to set out the proposed mitigation measures. An EIA may obviate the need for other more specific assessments. Where one is required, the information in the ES has to be taken into consideration when the LPA decides whether to grant permission. It may be helpful for a developer to request a 'screening opinion' from the LPA before submitting an application to determine whether an EIA is necessary. However, in cases where a full EIA is not required, the LPA may still require certain environmental information to be provided.

- *Flood risk assessment* (FRA). An FRA will be required for development proposals of 1 hectare or greater in Flood Zone 1 and for all proposals for new development located in Flood Zones 2 and 3 as designated by the Environment Agency (these zones may be shown in DPDs or on the Environment Agency's website). An FRA will also be required for any development other than minor development in a designated critical drainage area that has been notified to the LPA by the Environment Agency. The FRA should identify and assess the risks of all forms of flooding to and from the development and demonstrate how these flood risks will be managed, taking climate change into account. The FRA should identify opportunities to reduce the probability and consequences of flooding. The FRA should include the design of surface water management systems, including Sustainable Drainage Systems (SUDs), and address the requirement for safe access to and from the development in areas at risk of flooding. The FRA should be prepared by an applicant in consultation with the LPA with reference to its published Local Development Documents and any Strategic Flood Risk Assessment. The FRA should form part of an environmental statement when one is required. *PPS25: Development and Flood Risk* (2006) and its associated *Practice Guide* provide comprehensive guidance on carrying out FRAs and give advice on the responsibilities for controlling development where it might be directly affected by flooding or might affect flooding elsewhere.

- *Foul sewage and utilities assessment.* All new buildings need separate connections to foul and stormwater sewers. If an application proposes to connect a development to the existing drainage system then details of the existing system should be shown on the application drawing(s). It should be noted that in most circumstances surface water is not permitted to be connected to the public foul sewers. Where the development involves the disposal of trade waste or the disposal of foul sewage effluent other than to the public sewer, then a fuller foul drainage assessment will be required, including details of the method of storage, treatment and disposal. A foul drainage assessment should include a full appraisal of the site, its location and its suitability for storing, transporting and treating sewage. Where connection to the mains sewer is not practical then the foul/non-mains drainage assessment will be required to demonstrate why the development cannot connect to the public mains sewer system and show that the alternative means of disposal are satisfactory. Guidance on what should be included in a non-mains drainage assessment is given in *DETR Circular 03/99* and *Building Regulations 2000 Approved Document H* and in BS 6297:2007. If the proposed development results in any changes to or replacement of the existing system or the creation of a new system, scale plans of the new foul drainage arrangements will also need to be provided. This will include a location plan, cross-sections/elevations and specification. Drainage details that will achieve Building Regulations approval will be required. If connection to any of the above requires crossing land that is not in the applicant's ownership, other than a public highway, then notice may need to be served on the owners of that land. An application should indicate how the development connects to existing utility infrastructure systems. Most new development requires connection to existing utility services, including electricity and gas supplies, telecommunications and water supply, and also needs connection to foul and surface water drainage and disposal. Two planning issues arise; first, whether the existing services and infrastructure have sufficient capacity to accommodate the supply/service demands that would arise from the completed development, and second, whether the provision of services on site would give rise to any environmental impacts, such as excavations in the vicinity of trees or archaeological remains. The applicant should therefore demonstrate:

- that, following consultation with the service provider, the availability of utility services has been examined and that the proposals would not result in undue stress on the delivery of those services to the wider community
- that proposals incorporate any utility company requirements for substations, telecommunications equipment or similar structures
- that service routes have been planned to avoid, as far as possible, the potential for damage to trees and archaeological remains, and
- where the development impinges on existing infrastructure, that the provisions for relocating or protecting that infrastructure have been agreed with the service provider.

• *Heritage statement (including historical and archaeological features and scheduled ancient monuments)*. The scope and degree of detail necessary in a heritage statement will vary according to the particular circumstances of each application. You should therefore discuss your proposals with either a planning officer or a conservation officer before any application is made. The following is a guide to the sort of information that may be required for different types of application. For applications for listed building consent, a written statement that includes a schedule of works to the listed building(s), an analysis of the significance of archaeology, history and character of the building or structure, the principles of and justification for the proposed works and their impact on the special character of the listed building or structure, its setting and the setting of adjacent listed buildings may be required. A structural survey may be required in support of an application for listed building consent. For applications for conservation area consent, a written statement that includes a structural survey, an analysis of the character and appearance of the building or structure, the principles of and justification for the proposed demolition and its impact on the special character of the area may be required. For applications either related to or impacting on the setting of heritage assets, a written statement that includes plans showing any historic features that exist on or adjacent to the application site, including listed buildings and structures, historic parks and gardens, historic battlefields and scheduled ancient monuments, and an analysis of the significance of archaeology, history and character of the building or structure, the principles of and justification for the proposed works and their impact on the special character of the listed building or structure, its setting and the setting of adjacent listed buildings may be required. For applications within or adjacent to a conservation area, an assessment of the impact of the development on the character and appearance of the area may be required. For all applications involving the disturbance of ground within an Area of Archaeological Potential as defined in the development plan or in other areas in the case of a major development proposal or significant infrastructure works, an applicant may need to commission an assessment of existing archaeological information and submit the results as part of the heritage statement. For heritage assets, advice is provided in paragraphs 3.16 to 3.19 and 4.25 to 4.49 of *PPG15: Planning and the Historic Environment* (1994). For archaeological remains, advice is provided in *PPG16: Archaeology and Planning* (1990).

- *Land contamination assessment.* Applications may also need to be accompanied by a land contamination assessment, which should include an extended assessment of contamination in line with *PPG23: Planning and Pollution Control* (2004). Sufficient information should be required to determine the existence or otherwise of contamination, its nature and the risks it may pose and whether these can be satisfactorily reduced to an acceptable level. Where contamination is known or suspected or the proposed use would be particularly vulnerable, the applicant should provide such information with the application as is necessary to determine whether the proposed development can proceed.

- *Landfill applications*. Applicants should provide sufficient information to enable the waste planning authority to fulfil its requirements under the Landfill (England and Wales) Regulations 2002. This information may be provided as part of the ES.
- *Landscaping details*. Applications may be accompanied by landscaping details and include proposals for long-term maintenance and landscape management. There should be reference to landscaping and detailed landscaping proposals that follow from the design concept in the DAS, where one is required. Existing trees and other vegetation should, where practicable, be retained in new developments and protected during the construction of the development.
- *Lighting assessment*. Proposals involving the provision of publicly accessible developments, in the vicinity of residential property, involving a listed building or a conservation area, or in open countryside, where external lighting would be provided or made necessary by the development, should be required to be accompanied by details of external lighting and the proposed hours when the lighting would be switched on. These details should include a layout plan with beam orientation and a schedule of the equipment in the design. *Lighting in the Countryside: Towards good practice* (Countryside Commission, 1997) gives valuable guidance on what can be done to lessen the effects of external lighting and is applicable in towns as well as the countryside.
- *Noise assessment*. Applications for developments that raise issues of disturbance by noise to the occupants of nearby existing buildings, and for developments that are considered to be noise sensitive and which are close to existing sources of noise, should be supported by a noise assessment prepared by a suitably qualified acoustician. Further guidance is provided in *PPG24: Planning and Noise* (1994).
- *Open space assessment*. For development within open spaces, application proposals should be accompanied by plans showing any areas of existing or proposed open space within or adjoining the application site. Planning permission is not normally given for development of existing open spaces that local communities need. However, in the absence of a robust and up-to-date assessment by a local authority, an applicant may seek to demonstrate through an independent assessment that the land or buildings are surplus to local requirements. Any such evidence should accompany the

planning application. Here, 'open space' includes space falling within the definitions of that term in the Town and Country Planning Act 1990 or in *PPG17: Planning for Open Space, Sport and Recreation* (2002), which sets out national policy.

- *Parking provision.* Applications may be required to provide details of existing and proposed parking provision. These details could also be shown on a site layout plan.

- *Photographs, photomontages and models.* These provide useful background information and can help to show how large developments can be satisfactorily integrated within the street scene. Photographs should be provided if the proposal involves the demolition of an existing building or development affecting a conservation area or a listed building. The use of simple block models to show the proposed development within the context of its surroundings can also be very helpful, in our experience.

- *Planning obligations – draft head(s) of terms* (see *Planning obligations, developer contributions and 'planning gain'*, page 107). Where DPDs contain policies that give details of likely planning obligation requirements, an LPA may require a statement of the proposed heads of terms to be submitted with the application. Applicants should clarify the LPA's requirements in pre-application discussions. Further advice is available in *ODPM Circular 05/2005: Planning Obligations,* and a model section 106 agreement (as revised on 15 August 2006) is available on the CLG website.

- *Planning statement.* A planning statement identifies the context and need for a proposed development and includes an assessment of how the proposed development accords with relevant national, regional and local planning policies. It may also include details of consultations with the LPA and with wider community and statutory consultees undertaken prior to submission. Alternatively, a separate statement on community involvement may also be appropriate. In our experience, planning statements are best prepared by a professional planning consultant, and should stress the benefits of the development and argue the case for permission. They may be combined with or incorporate a DAS. Such a report can often be key in influencing a successful outcome.

- *Site waste management plan.* Proposed new development should be supported by site waste management plans of the type encouraged by the code of practice *Site Waste Management Plans: Guidance for construction contractors and clients,* published in 2004 by the Department of Trade and

Industry (now the Department for Business, Innovation and Skills). These are intended to encourage the identification of the volume and type of material to be demolished and/or excavated and opportunities for the reuse and recovery of materials, and to demonstrate how off-site disposal of waste will be minimised and managed.

- *Statement of Community Involvement (SCI)*. Applications may need to be supported by a statement setting out how the applicant has complied with the requirements for pre-application consultation set out in the LPA's adopted SCI and demonstrating that the views of the local community have been sought and taken into account in the formulation of development proposals.

- *Structural survey.* A structural survey may be required in support of an application if the proposal involves substantial demolition, such as for barn conversion applications.

- *Telecommunications development.* Planning applications for mast and antenna development by mobile phone network operators in England should be accompanied by a range of supplementary information, including the area of search, details of any consultation undertaken, details of the proposed structure, and technical justification and information about the proposed development. Planning applications should also be accompanied by a signed declaration that the equipment and installation have been designed to be in full compliance with the requirements of the radio frequency public exposure guidelines of the International Commission on Non-Ionizing Radiation Protection. Further guidance on the information that may be required is set out in the *Code of Best Practice on Mobile Network Development* (ODPM, 2002).

- *Town centre uses (evidence to accompany applications).* PPS6: Planning for *Town Centres* (2005) sets out in paragraph 1.8 the main town centre uses to which the policy applies. Subject to the policies set out in the document, paragraph 3.4 lists the key considerations for which applicants should present evidence. The level and type of evidence and analysis required to address the key considerations should be proportionate to the scale and nature of the proposal.

- *Transport assessment* (TA). *PPG13: Transport* (2001) advises that a TA should be submitted as part of any planning application where the proposed develop-ment has significant transport implications. The coverage and detail of the TA should reflect the scale of the development and the extent of the transport implications of the proposal. For smaller schemes, the TA should simply outline the transport aspects of the application, while for major proposals the TA should illustrate accessibility to the site by all modes of transport, and the likely modal split of journeys to and from the site. The TA should also give details of proposed measures to improve access by public transport, walking and cycling, to reduce the need for parking associated with the proposal and to mitigate transport impacts. Further guidance may be found in *Guidance on Transport Assessment* (DfT, 2007).

- *Travel plan.* The travel plan (sometimes called a 'green travel' or 'commuter' plan) promotes sustainable travel choices, for example walking, cycling, public transport or car sharing, as an alternative to single occupancy car journeys. A travel plan should be submitted with planning applications that are likely to have significant transport implications, as advised by *PPG13: Transport* (2001), paragraphs 87 to 91. Further advice is available in *Good Practice Guidelines: Delivering travel plans through the planning process* (DfT, 2009).

- *Tree survey/arboricultural implications.* Where there are trees within the application site, or on land adjacent to it that could influence or be affected by the development (including street trees), information will be required on which trees are to be retained and on the means of protecting these trees during construction works. This information should be prepared by a qualified arboriculturist. Full guidance on the survey information, protection plan and method statement that should be provided with an application is set out in BS 5837:2005 *Trees in Relation to Construction – Recommendations*. Using the methodology set out in the BS should help to ensure that development is suitably integrated with trees and that potential conflicts are avoided.

- *Ventilation/extraction statement.* Details of the position and design of ventilation and extraction equipment, including odour abatement techniques and acoustic characteristics, will be required to accompany all applications for the use of premises for purposes within use classes A3 (restaurants and cafes – use for the sale of food and drink for consumption on the premises), A4 (drinking establishments – use as a public house, wine-bar or other drinking establishment), A5 (hot-food takeaways – use for the sale of hot food for consumption off the premises), B1 (general business) and B2 (general industrial). This information (excluding odour abatement techniques unless specifically required) will also be required for significant retail, business, industrial or leisure or other similar developments where substantial ventilation or extraction equipment is proposed to be installed, for example for hot-food takeaways, restaurant uses and laundrettes.

Although not on the national list of additional information that LPAs may require, from recent experience we would add that LPAs may also request the submission of the following information:

- *Sustainability assessment* – outlining the key elements of the scheme that address sustainable development issues, such as the positive environmental, social and economic implications, including those considered during a Building Research Establishment Environmental Assessment Method (BREEAM) assessment. BREEAM is the leading and most widely used environmental assessment method for buildings and sets the standard for best practice in sustainable design. It has become the de facto measure used to describe a building's environmental performance.
- *Energy statement* – showing the predicted energy demand of the proposed development and the degree to which the development meets current 'green building' requirements for reducing carbon dioxide emissions by onsite renewable energy generation. Such a statement may form part of a sustainability or BREEAM assessment. Further advice is available in *PPS22: Renewable Energy* (2004) and in *Planning Policy Statement: Planning and Climate Change – Supplement to Planning Policy Statement 1* (2007).
- *Construction/demolition management plan* – outlining arrangements for the parking of vehicles of site operatives and visitors; loading and unloading of plant and materials; storage of plant and materials used in constructing the development; the erection and maintenance of any security hoarding; wheel-washing facilities; the control of dust emissions and dirt during construction; and a scheme for recycling/disposing of waste resulting from demolition and construction works.
- *Crime prevention report* – explaining how the development incorporates measures to safeguard community safety. See *Safer Places: The planning system and crime prevention* (ODPM, 2004).

If your application needs to be accompanied by any additional information, it may be advisable to provide additional copies as this will assist consultation with others and avoid unnecessary delays. Always ask that one set is placed with the public copy of the application and that the contents of any written material, especially the DAS or overarching planning statement, are reported to members of the committee that will consider the application.

At Appendix E we have included our own checklist of the main considerations relating to major proposals. However, this should be treated with some caution as it cannot, of course, anticipate every circumstance.

Because of concerns expressed by many in the development industry on the exponential growth in paperwork now necessary to ensure that an application is validated and processed, and in response to the recommendations in the Killian Pretty Review, the government is proposing to issue revised guidance that would cut down information requirements, as discussed above under the heading *Best practice on the validation of planning applications*, at page 78.

What happens to your application and what should you do?

Registration

Once an application has been received, it is checked to see whether it is complete (that is, valid) and a letter of acknowledgement is sent to the applicant (although the letter does not necessarily confirm that the application is valid). As we have just outlined, the government has issued best practice guidance on the validation of planning applications, and the compliance or otherwise with this will be an important consideration. Normally, most minor and small-scale applications should be validated within three to five working days from the date of receipt. Major applications should be validated within ten working days.

Sometimes the planning authority will amend the description of the proposed development to ensure that it accurately reflects what is shown on the submitted drawings. So this should be checked and any concerns taken up immediately with the case officer identified in the letter as dealing with the application. The acknowledgement letter will also give a reference number (which should always be quoted in correspondence) and the time period within which the planning authority intends to make a decision. This is normally eight weeks, although will be longer for major applications (13 weeks) and applications that require an environmental statement (16 weeks). These decision-making periods start to run from the day *after* the day on which a valid application with the correct fee is received by a local authority, irrespective of whether the application is submitted electronically or in paper format. However, the period for determining your application may be subsequently extended by the planning authority with your written agreement.

Regardless of the type of application, if it has not been decided by the planning authority within the relevant statutory time limit and you have not agreed to extend this, you have a right of appeal against the application's 'non-determination'.

An invalid application may be returned, or it may be retained and a request issued for identified deficiencies to be rectified. If the deficiencies are not remedied within a specified period, the application will then be returned. The most common reasons cited for not validating applications, which obviously you must avoid, include:

- use of the wrong copy of 1APP or an old form
- forms submitted without signatures
- failure to provide correct certificates (in particular the agricultural holdings certificate)
- no redline boundary on drawings
- insufficient information, and a failure to realise that the information require-ments set out in local validation lists needed to be met for an application to be valid
- submitted drawings showing insufficient detail or that are inconsistent
- different application addresses on the forms and drawings
- building works encroaching on neighbouring property
- incorrectly signed or unsigned certificates
- insufficient copies of plans or forms
- inconsistency between elevations and floor plans
- incorrect fees enclosed or fee cheque not signed.

Remember that the planning authority will not start to consider the application until it is valid, so it is essential that all the necessary documentation is in order. Through the government's housing and planning delivery grant scheme, plan-ning authorities are rewarded for making improvements to or meeting best value targets for their performance in handling planning applications, so this often acts as a significant disincentive for accepting applications unless and until authorities are fully satisfied that everything is in place. And, of course, the desire to be rewarded for meeting the government's targets can often influ-ence the way and speed with which your application is subsequently considered!

If a planning authority refuses to validate your application, you can appeal against this to the Secretary of State. There is no mechanism for resolving disputes over the calculation of the application fee (a common problem in our experience) other than to lodge an appeal. In order to accept the appeal, the Planning Inspectorate must first consider whether the correct fee has been paid and the application is valid (see CLG Circular 04/2008).

Once the application is deemed to be valid it will be registered (that is, entered on the public planning register), and recorded in the planning authority's computer system. The respective copies of the application are separated and one is made up into a working file, which is then allocated to the case officer, normally with details of any previous planning history on the site. One copy is made available for public inspection at the reception desk. The remaining copies will be used for other consultation purposes.

Publicity and consultations

Practice on publicising applications varies, but minimum requirements are set out in the GDPO and explained in DoE Circular 15/92. Currently, applications must be publicised by way of a notice in a local newspaper, a site notice or by neighbour notification letter. The precise form of publicity is determined by the regulations, and different types of application require different methods of statutory publicity. The planning authority has a duty to take into account all representations received before determining the application. A period of 21 days is normally given for comments (14 days where advertised), although the planning authority is not precluded from considering comments made after this time has expired.

Special provisions apply for publicising major developments and applications affecting conservation areas and listed buildings, and for notifying the Secretary of State of 'departure applications' (that is, those conflicting with the development plan and that an authority is minded to approve) and of development within the Green Belt, outside town centres, within World Heritage sites, on playing fields or within flood risk areas, in certain circumstances (these are defined in CLG Circular 02/2009). According to the type and scale of the proposed development, planning authorities are required to consult specified persons or bodies (so-called 'statutory consultees'), such as the highway authority, the Environment Agency, local parish or community council, various government authorities and agencies, or other organisations and third parties. Internally, the planning authority might well consult its colleagues in other departments, such as in environmental protection, drainage or leisure services. Under measures introduced in August 2005, statutory consultees on planning applications are required to respond within 21 days.

A consultation document proposing revised arrangements for publicising planning applications within England was published by CLG in July 2009.

Assessment of the application

The planning officer will identify the issues arising from the proposed development, assess the application against relevant development plan policies, Supplementary Planning Guidance and SPDs, and any other considerations, and invariably carry out an inspection of the site (although there is no statutory obligation to do this). Further information on the application may be requested or minor amendments sought. However, because of the need for LPAs to process applications efficiently, within the required time limits, material changes to the proposed development to overcome post-submission concerns may be resisted. In these circumstances, the LPA may suggest that the application be withdrawn and insist on a fresh application, which may or may not benefit from the 'free go' fee exemption.

In any event, it is always prudent to monitor progress on the application closely and to speak to the planning officer about four to five weeks after it has been submitted, as by this time they should have an idea of any

"Monitor progress on the application closely"

issues that might need to be addressed and whether the application is one that will need to be reported to committee or can be decided by officers under delegated powers. Such powers vary widely and will be set out in the council's constitution, which can be inspected where required.

See also:
Negotiations
and tactics,
page 101

In response to any negotiations with relevant officers, it might be necessary to modify the proposal slightly and submit revised drawings. These will normally trigger a further but shorter period of public consultation (usually 14 days).

Once the relevant consultation periods have expired and comments have been considered, and the planning officer is satisfied that it is appropriate to do so, they may then determine the application under delegated powers or, if the application falls outside the scope of such powers, prepare a written report and recommendation for consideration by council members. Inevitably, the extent of the planning officer's workload and relevant performance targets will have a bearing on when the application might be decided, with the former being the most common reason for delay.

Reports are usually prepared about two weeks before the date of the committee meeting. As this often acts as an informal deadline for submitting any outstanding details or information, such material should be provided well in advance, otherwise the planning officer may decide to hold the application in abeyance until the following meeting. The planning officer's report may be the subject of internal consultation and so may need to be cleared by more senior officers in the management hierarchy.

It is important to try to establish when and how an application is to be decided as, according to how well things have been going, this will affect possible courses of action. For example, if it is clear that the planning officer is opposed to the application and is likely to refuse it under delegated powers, you might wish to consider asking a council member to intervene and request that the application be reported to committee, if this is possible. Among other things, this would enable relevant council members to be lobbied or, where such opportunities exist, allow you to address the committee in person.

Planning officers' reports

Planning reports to the relevant committee, which will usually sit every three to four weeks or so, should be open and impartial. Most follow the same format and, where appropriate, include a summary of:

- the proposed development and any related background information
- the site and its surroundings
- relevant planning history
- relevant development plan provisions
- consultations carried out, comments received, views expressed in letters of objection or support, details of any petition and so forth
- the main issues and planning considerations
- a recommendation to grant or refuse permission

- draft conditions to be imposed, with reasons (however, these may be abbreviated using the planning authority's own particular codes)
- the terms of any planning obligation to be sought
- draft reasons for refusal or grant of permission.

In accordance with freedom of information legislation, the planning officer's report to committee and related background papers (that is, the planning application file) must be made available for public inspection at least five clear working days before the date of the committee meeting. Many authorities exceed the minimum requirements. It is always advisable to obtain a copy of the report as soon as it is available, which is usually possible by speaking to the relevant committee clerk or the member services department. Agenda papers and reports are now generally available on councils' websites.

There are important benefits of getting hold of the planning officer's report:

- It will enable you to check the planning officer's advice and recommendation and to confirm that any negotiations have succeeded and that any informal assurances given by the planning authority have been fulfilled. Make sure that relevant matters have been understood and are adequately summarised, that nothing important has been omitted and that the report is not misleading. In some instances, a case officer's own views might have been overruled or modified in some way by more senior officers. However, while this is quite legitimate, it is normal practice to notify the applicant beforehand of any significant change, to avoid any nasty surprises.
- It will reveal the nature and extent of any local opposition or objections raised by any major third parties, if these have not already been disclosed.
- It will provide you with the information you need to lobby in support of the proposal, if this is necessary. As council members will now be aware of the planning officer's advice, they are better briefed and so are often more willing to discuss the application, although many will not express a view for fear of prejudicing consideration of the application at the committee meeting. This is also the time when lobbying by third parties steps up a gear and is likely to be most effective.
- It will enable last minute action or negotiations to try to resolve outstanding issues and rectify mistakes, and so possibly avoid a refusal.
- It will allow you to consider any conditions, the need for developer contributions or requirements of any planning obligation, and any reasons for refusal.

When faced with the prospect of refusal

If the application is recommended for refusal, your choices are as follows:

- Let the application run and perhaps lobby members (councillors) in the hope that they will overturn the recommendation.
- Withdraw the application, to avoid 'negative history', and perhaps consider preparing a revised proposal (which in certain circumstances would be exempt from a fresh application fee).
- Ask for the application to be deferred to enable further negotiations to take place. However, most planning authorities are reluctant to do this unless the application has already failed to be decided within the statutory period and there is some clear evidence of an intention to overcome relevant objections, or if revised drawings have been received by the planning authority too late for them to be considered properly.

Knowing whether, when best, or how much to lobby council members during the application process can be quite hard to judge. This is a sensitive matter that requires great care, not least because it could antagonise officers involved in the application or appear to undermine delicate negotiations.

Too much lobbying can put off decision-makers. None might mean that a valuable opportunity is missed to stress the benefits of a proposed development. Too little could, of course, prove ineffective!

Lobbying can include letters addressed to individual councillors or speaking directly with key council members, such as the ward member and the chair and vice-chair of the planning committee. Often lobbying is more successful when conducted by the applicant, as it may be thought to be more heartfelt than when coming from an agent who is 'simply going through the motions'. However, large-scale or complex proposals may well require advice from a planning consultant or specialist public relations consultant.

Many authorities have adopted a members' code of practice on planning procedures, setting out some basic principles on lobbying to ensure that members maintain their impartiality and do not appear to 'fetter their discretion' in the decision-making process. So, you should try to get hold of a copy of this, where available. Codes may discourage direct approaches to members in favour of a public speaking system (see below) or discourage members from expressing a view before an

See also: Negotiations and tactics, page 101

application is formally considered, unless it is made clear that it is a personal opinion that does not bind the council. Codes may instead encourage information to be shared with, or put in writing to, officers.

At worst, allowing an application to run and be considered by the council members will preserve the right of appeal, which is lost once an application is withdrawn. In any event, a revised application submitted within 12 months will not require a new fee, provided the proposed development is of the same character or description as that which was the subject of the original application and it is submitted by the same applicant. The planning authority is able, however, to decline to accept repeat applications in certain circumstances (see the seventh bullet point on page 103 on aggressive tactics).

At the committee meeting

Many planning authorities have introduced procedures for public speaking at committee meetings, following prior notification, but this is generally limited to about three minutes per speaker. Nevertheless, this may be long enough to stress the main benefits of the proposed development and/or respond briefly to comments made by objectors. But it is doubtful in the majority of cases whether such action is pivotal in changing the outcome of the application. Regardless of whether any public speaking rights exist, it is usually a good idea to attend the committee meeting to listen to any discussion as that might explain relevant issues and could inform any resubmission or appeal that might be lodged.

In addition to considering the planning officer's written report, at the meeting of the planning committee its members may receive an oral presentation from key officers, often aided by visual material such as photographs and plans, and this will be supplemented by any late information received since the report was prepared. According to member interest and how complex or controversial an application is, decisions will either be made 'on the nod' (that is, in accordance with the officer's recommendation and with no discussion of the application) or after some discussion and a subsequent vote.

Taking the decision

Council members are not bound to follow the advice of their professional advisers, but they must be able to demonstrate good reasons based on land-use planning grounds for not doing so or else they will be liable for an award of costs on appeal. Typically, fewer than 10 per cent of recommendations are over-turned. In some cases, the committee might defer making a decision in order to request further information or amendments from the applicant, advice from its officers, or more consultations to be carried out. Alternatively, it might wish to look at the site itself before making a decision, or to instruct a sub-committee to do this on its behalf and report back to its next meeting with a recommendation. Although practice varies, in such circumstances it is common to invite interested parties to be present, and there may be opportunities for speaking for or against the proposal.

Decisions made on certain applications, particularly those involving significant policy issues, may need to be referred to other committees or boards of the council, or to a meeting of the full council itself.

Following its consideration of an application, generally the committee will resolve to do one of the following things:

- grant unconditional permission/approval/consent
- grant permission/approval/consent with conditions
- grant permission following the prior completion of a planning obligation
- refuse permission
- defer a decision on the application.

Figure 5.1 (page 102) summarises what happens to an application after it has been submitted to the local planning authority.

Negotiations and tactics

Depending on the scale and complexity of the proposed development, at some stage in the planning process it is likely that negotiations will be necessary; whether to address matters of concern or, where necessary, to try to overcome objections raised by either the planning authority or other interested parties. Because of the target-driven culture of decision-making that has been introduced in recent years, once applications have been submitted the scope for negotiations at this stage is now generally limited. Instead, most negotiations take place either before an application has been made, or after one has been refused in order to try to pave the way for a revised proposal. Clearly, successful negotiations often depend on the skill and experience of those involved. The following are some tips:

FIGURE 5.1: *Stages in processing a planning application*

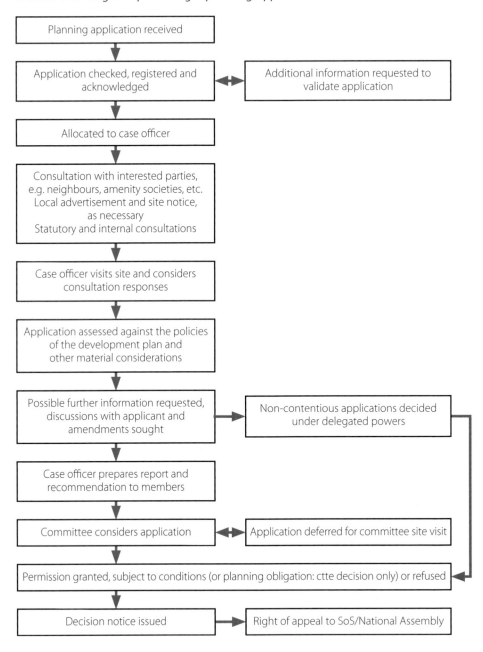

- Make sure that you negotiate with the right people. Identify the key players in the process, both within the authority (who are likely to include officers from various departments) and outside (such as the highway authority or the Environment Agency). For bigger schemes, many local authorities now provide a development team approach, with a single point of contact. Unless the proposed development is one that is likely to raise significant or district-wide issues, it will rarely be necessary to start at the top (although bigger schemes are likely to be handled by more senior officers, in any event). However, where appropriate, a quick telephone call to the council's head of development management will establish who is likely to deal with relevant matters. Most development management officers work in teams dealing with particular geographical areas.

- Find out something about the political composition of the council, which group holds power, what the major drivers are (for example, economic regeneration, maintenance of the Green Belt or affordable housing provision). Does the planning authority operate within a corporate culture where development is positively encouraged, managed or generally resisted? Establish who are the key councillors that you might wish to speak with, including the relevant committee chair and ward members. Beware of over-lobbying as this can be counterproductive. (See also the advice above on lobbying, page 99.)

- Lobbying MPs or government departments is rarely effective, and may backfire if the matter becomes a political hot potato.

- Establish who is likely to object to the proposed development (such as local amenity groups) and whether there is anything that can be done to reduce or overcome any opposition.

- Confrontation sometimes has its place in the planning process. However, a partnership approach, developing good working relationships and seeking to understand the needs and aspirations of the authority and others – and involving

"Above all, be realistic in your expectations!"

them in the project – are more likely to be effective. Above all, be realistic in your expectations!

- Neither planning officers nor elected members respond well to threats, including suggestions that any refusal will be appealed.

- Aggressive tactics, such as 'twin-tracking' (that is, submitting identical applications simultaneously with the objective of lodging an appeal for non-determination of one while continuing to negotiate on the other), can waste local authority resources and cause confusion. This particular tactic is outlawed under the 2004 Act. The Act also extends a planning authority's ability to decline to accept repeat applications that are intended to wear down its resistance to development. In addition to declining to determine an application that is the same as or very similar to one that has either been refused within the previous two years or dismissed on appeal, an authority is able to refuse to determine an application where it has refused two similar applications and there has been no appeal lodged in the preceding two-year period.

- Similarly, it can be counterproductive to submit an application that you know to be 'overdevelopment' (for example because it includes too many housing units) simply because you are trying to maximise the development potential of a site but are expecting during the course of negotiations to reduce its scale (and in so doing wish to appear to have made significant concessions). Planning authorities are unlikely to negotiate in such circumstances and will often refuse blatantly unacceptable applications quickly, especially if matters flagged-up during any pre-application discussions have been ignored.

- Stress any benefits of the development. Where a proposed development is likely to be acceptable in any event, it will seldom be necessary to consider any 'planning gain'. However, where a proposed development is likely to be regarded as contrary to policy, it is essential to demonstrate 'other considerations' sufficient to override such objections.

- Consider the use of other consultants and specialists. Local authorities often respond more positively in planner-to-planner negotiations, especially where there is already a good working relationship. In addition, planning officers will normally discuss matters more openly and freely where the client is not directly involved in negotiations.

- Two powerful negotiating tools that development management officers have at their disposal are bluff and delay. Knowing when planning officers are seeking to achieve their objectives by making unreasonable demands or merely expressing personal preferences requires experience and a detailed knowledge of the council's policies and national planning guidelines. However, acceding to some requests for changes to a scheme or for a planning obligation may often be better, on balance, than suffering the financial consequences of a significant delay in achieving permission.

- Before meetings with the planning authority, make sure that you and any other participants are well briefed. Establish beforehand which matters are 'negotiable' and might be conceded and which ones cannot. At the end of any discussions, be clear as to what has been agreed and points for action.

- Do not rely solely on discussions. Make sure that notes of meetings are kept and that the planning authority receives subsequent correspondence detailing what has been agreed. Remember that others may look at the application file or background papers, particularly in the event of an appeal or any challenge.
- Check the wording of draft conditions and the terms of any obligations; where necessary, engage the services of specialists to do this.

Decision notices

The courts have ruled that the date of a decision is when the relevant notice is issued, and not when any committee has resolved to either grant or refuse permission. As it may take planning authorities several days after the resolution to issue a notice, if time is of the essence it may well pay you to chase them up for this.

Decision notices must state clearly and precisely the planning authority's full reasons for refusing or granting permission or for any condition imposed; most planning authorities use standard reasons for refusal and conditions to deal with regularly encountered issues. Any planning policies that have been relied upon should also be identified in the notice.

Some planning authorities will attach a list of 'informatives' to the decision notice. These do not form part of the decision itself but are notes setting out guidance on related matters, such as the need for other statutory consents or, in the case of a refusal, some indication of the kind of development the planning authority would find acceptable.

Planning conditions

It is essential to consider carefully any conditions attached to a permission as, unless appealed, they will be deemed to have been accepted and may be enforced by the planning authority by means of a breach of condition notice, against which there is no right of appeal.

See also: Breaches of planning control, page 137

The general approach to conditions is that they should be imposed only where there is a clear land-use planning justification. The companion guide to PPS1 (*The*

Planning System: General Principles) explains that the key test for whether a particular condition is necessary is if planning permission would have to be refused if the condition were not imposed.

Detailed advice on conditions is set out in *DoE Circular 11/95: The Use of Conditions in Planning Permissions*, as amended by ODPM Circular 08/2005 and, in respect of negative conditions, revised by ODPM letter dated 25 November 2002. Among other things, the circular explains that conditions should only be imposed where they are:

- necessary
- relevant to planning
- relevant to the development to be permitted
- enforceable
- precise
- reasonable in all other respects.

These criteria are examined in the circular, and examples are given of conditions that are acceptable and ones that are not. Conditions can be imposed to deal with matters such as access, parking, landscaping, noise and restrictions on hours of use.

Generally, conditions should only be imposed on land under the control of the applicant, whether within or outside the site, although it is possible to impose a negative or 'Grampian' condition (so-called after the case of *Grampian Regional Council v. City of Aberdeen District Council* [1984] JPL 590 where such an approach was held to be acceptable). This prevents the commencement of development until a specified action (such as a road improvement) has taken place. However, when there are no prospects at all of the action in question being performed within the life of the permission, it is the Secretary of State's policy that negative conditions should not be imposed. In other words, in circumstances when the interested third party has said that they have no intention of carrying out the action or allowing it to be carried out.

Notwithstanding the principle that planning controls are not normally concerned with the identity of the user and that planning permission runs with the land, in exceptional circumstances conditions may be imposed to make a permission personal to the applicant. This sometimes happens where, for example, a particular business use is considered of special importance to the local economy, but which in any other circumstances would be considered unacceptable. In addition, conditions may be imposed to restrict the occupation of a building, for example in the case of agricultural dwellings or staff accommodation.

Government advice to planning authorities is that generally conditions should be used in preference to planning obligations.

Following consultation with the Planning Officers Society, the Planning Inspectorate has published a list of model conditions to supplement those in DoE Circular 11/95. These may be viewed on the Planning Inspectorate's website. The government has also indicated that the guidance in the circular needs updating. It is carrying out a comprehensive review of current practice on how conditions are used and discharged, prior to publishing revised guidance.

Planning obligations, developer contributions and 'planning gain'

Although not defined in planning law or guidance, 'planning gain' is a somewhat misleading and increasingly unfashionable expression; it essentially refers to the community benefits or safeguards that are provided by a development. These are usually at the developer's expense and achieved by means of a planning obligation (also – although not entirely correctly – frequently called a 'section 106 agreement', as it is made under section 106 of the 1990 Act).

A planning obligation is a deed that is legally binding on subsequent owners. It is usually created by agreement with the LPA (a 'planning agreement'). However, it may also be offered unilaterally by a developer, particularly on appeal when a developer considers that unreasonable demands are being made by the planning authority (a 'unilateral undertaking'). The obligation may be positive, requiring something to be done, or negative, preventing something from happening. They may thus:

- restrict development or the use of land in a particular way
- require operations or activities to be carried out in, on, under or over land
- require the land to be used in a specified way
- require financial contributions to be made to the authority.

Like planning conditions, planning obligations may be used to allow development that might otherwise be refused. They must, however, only be sought where they are:

- necessary
- relevant to planning
- directly related to the proposed development
- fairly and reasonably related in scale and kind to the proposed development
- reasonable in all other respects.

Anyone with an interest in the land may enter into an obligation, which will only take effect once the planning permission is granted and implemented.

In the main, planning obligations are used to secure developer contributions to ensure that a developer provides, pays for or contributes to new or improved infrastructure or community facilities that would not have been necessary but for their development. Some common examples include:

- affordable housing
- access/highways/transport arrangements
- car parking
- public open space
- social, educational, recreational, sporting or other community provision

provided that the need for these arises directly from the development or is required to offset or replace the loss of existing resources or facilities on the site.

In line with ODPM Circular 05/2005, which gives relevant policy guidance, many authorities have published SPDs setting out formulae and standard charges that will apply to certain types of development or to amounts of development above a specified threshold.

Obligations are sometimes used to restrict the occupancy of land and buildings (such as to agricultural workers, or those of retirement age in the case of sheltered housing schemes), to require the giving up of existing use rights or planning permissions or to ensure the provision of affordable housing.

Government advice is that conditions imposed on a planning permission should not be repeated in a planning obligation (as this frustrates a developer's right to appeal), although many planning authorities will often try to do this. When dealing with planning agreements, it is essential to seek advice from a planning solicitor or planning consultant.

Where a planning obligation no longer serves any land-use planning objective it may, on application to the planning authority, be discharged by agreement between the authority and the interested parties against whom it is enforceable. Similarly, a planning obligation may be modified with the consent of the planning authority, where it would serve a useful planning purpose equally well with some modification proposed by the applicant. In the case of a planning authority's failure to determine an application to modify or discharge an obligation, or its decision to refuse such an application, there is a right of appeal to the Secretary of State.

Planning obligations may be enforced through the courts by means of an injunction.

Further advice on this complex subject is set out for England in *ODPM Circular 05/ 2005: Planning Obligations*, and for Wales in *WO Circular 13/97: Planning Obligations*. See also the CLG publication *Planning Obligations: Practice guidance*, published in August 2006, which aims to provide LPAs and developers with practical tools and methods to help improve the development, negotiation and implementation of planning obligations. A model section 106 agreement has been published on the CLG website. In addition, the Planning Inspectorate's website includes a checklist for planning obligations, together with a glossary of common terms used in such obligations.

As part of its planning reforms, the government has made several attempts to improve the system of planning obligations and developer contributions to make it simpler, more certain and fairer. The controversial recommendation in the final report of the Barker Review of Housing Supply (HM Treasury, March 2004) for a charge to be imposed when planning permission is granted was omitted from the Planning Act 2008 amid widespread opposition to the idea.

The Planning Act 2008 makes provision for a so-called 'Community Infrastructure Levy' (CIL). This will be a new charge that local authorities in England and Wales will be empowered, but not required, to levy on most types of new development in their area. CIL charges will be based on simple formulae that relate the amount of the charge to the size and character of the development paying it. The CIL will be levied on buildings rather than development. Householder development and non-residential development beneath a threshold of $100 \, m^2$ will not be liable. Payment will be due at the commencement of development and not when planning permission is granted. It is proposed that the proceeds of the levy will be spent on local and sub-regional infrastructure to support the development of the area. The new discretionary charge will come into force in April 2010. Following the introduction of the CIL, the government aims to restrict the use of planning obligations, but this will not have retrospective effect. It is also to consider any necessary changes that might be required to guidance or policy on planning obligations.

SUMMARY

- As an architect, your day-to-day dealings with planning authorities will most likely mean the submission of applications and trying to secure permission for your proposals. It is therefore vital that you understand the processes and the people involved, and know where to look for extra guidance. Remember that the role of planning is entirely different from that of the Building Regulations regime and a grant of planning permission does not override the need for any other consent that may be necessary.
- The term 'development' includes both operational development and changes of use.
- Not all development requires planning permission from the LPA. 'Permitted development', as defined by the General Permitted Development Order, avoids the need to apply for such permission. However, permitted development rights may be restricted by national or local designations.
- Local Development Orders and Simplified Planning Zones may be in force, again affecting the need for planning permission.
- When assessing the need for planning permission, be cautious: check with a planning officer.
- Pre-application discussions can greatly help when preparing applications by identifying early on any planning issues that may affect the proposed scheme. LPAs are now often reluctant to negotiate after an application has been submitted, therefore such discussions have become increasingly important.
- There are various types of planning applications, including those for outline permission, reserved matters approval, full permission, retrospective permission and the variation or removal of conditions. Be sure you understand the differences, which permissions you need and what you have been granted.
- In addition to planning permission, special consents may be required for particular forms of development, such as those affecting listed buildings or within conservation areas.
- Certificates of Lawfulness may be obtained in some situations, confirming that certain existing or proposed activities or developments are or would be lawful and therefore do not need planning permission.

- The preparation of planning applications can be complex, and small mistakes or omissions of information can lead to applications being deemed invalid. The key to successful planning applications is careful preparation and presentation.
- Follow the advice on preparing applications issued by the government, check the LPA's own validation requirements, and make sure that applications include all the necessary information. LPAs may require many separate impact assessments, statements, maps and drawings.
- The process of assessing and deciding an application can be long and drawn out, and many people may be involved on the way to the final decision. Make sure you understand the process and can identify the key players so that you will know who to approach for advice and who you can lobby for support. Remember: lobbying and negotiation are skills – you should exploit any opportunities to push your proposal, but be careful not to antagonise decision-makers.
- Planning permissions may come with conditions attached or require the prior completion of a planning obligation. Make sure you understand their implications and are clear about what is required.
- Know your limitations; be prepared to use other specialists such as a planning consultant in appropriate circumstances!

Section 6
Going to appeal, challenges and complaints

In this Section:

- *Planning appeals*
- *Challenges: statutory and judicial reviews*
- *Complaints to the council or Ombudsman*
- *Human rights*

Planning appeals

An appeal should be an act of last resort and be considered only when all else has failed. Nevertheless, from time to time circumstances might arise where it is necessary to appeal against a planning authority's decision or its failure to determine an application.

Appeals are made to the Secretary of State. In England, this means the Secretary of State for Communities and Local Government, and in Wales, the National Assembly. The appeals process itself is handled by the Planning Inspectorate (often abbreviated to PINS), a quasi-autonomous executive agency that is responsible for its own day-to-day management, and which reports to the Secretary of State and the Welsh Assembly Government. Its role is governed by the three 'Franks' principles:

- openness
- fairness
- impartiality.

Its inspectors come from a variety of backgrounds, including planning, architecture, the environment, law and engineering. They are carefully selected, undergo rigorous training and work from home, with the support of office-based staff at the Inspectorate's headquarters in Bristol (or in Cardiff, where appeals are dealt with on behalf of the National Assembly for Wales).

Jurisdiction for determining appeals is generally 'transferred' from the Secretary of State to inspectors, who are therefore responsible for determining (that is, deciding) most ordinary planning appeals. However, the Secretary of State retains the power to 'recover' jurisdiction in certain prescribed circumstances, such as where an appeal involves a large, complex or controversial development or where a government department has raised major objections. This power is exercised rarely and accounts for no more than about 2 per cent of all appeal decisions.

Where jurisdiction is recovered, the decision will be made after consideration of a written report and recommendation from an inspector, following a local inquiry. But whether it is the Secretary of State or the National Assembly for Wales, or inspectors who ultimately determine a planning appeal, they must justify their decision and take into account:

• national, regional and local planning policy
• relevant planning issues and material considerations
• the views of third parties.

Right of appeal

A disappointed *applicant* may lodge an appeal against:

• the refusal of permission
• conditions on a permission or reserved matters approval that are considered unacceptable
• the refusal to approve details submitted as a reserved matter, following the grant of an outline permission
• the refusal to approve details arising from a condition of any planning permission
• any requirement to submit further details in support of an outline application
• the planning authority's failure to decide an application within the prescribed time period, unless this is extended by agreement.

In addition, there are rights of appeal in respect of:

- removal or variation of conditions attached to an existing permission
- listed building consent
- conservation area consent
- advertisement regulations consent
- Tree Preservation Order consent
- hedgerow regulations consent
- Certificates of Lawfulness ('lawful development certificates')
- enforcement notices.

The person (or party) that makes the appeal is called the 'appellant'.

Whether it is an appeal against a planning refusal or some other special consent or decision, the broad issues that any appellant should consider and the general principles and procedures involved are similar. However, it should be noted that the time limits for lodging an appeal vary.

In common with other parts of the planning system, the appeals process has been the subject of recent reform. The most notable changes include: the introduction of a fast-track Householder Appeals Service (HAS); the removal of an appellant's right to be heard, with the Inspectorate deciding the method of appeal; and the imminent introduction of an appeal fee. We describe these changes in more detail later.

Unlike some other planning jurisdictions, for example in Ireland and the Isle of Man, there is no third party right of appeal against a planning authority's decision to grant permission (although this may be challenged by judicial review, as explained later).

Deciding whether to appeal

Even in a seemingly straightforward case, for example where there has been consistent officer support for the proposed development and it has been recommended for approval, but this has subsequently been overturned by council members, it is probably best to seek an independent opinion on the chances of success and other advice from an appropriate specialist, such as a planning consultant. But before doing that, it is crucial to study carefully the reasons for refusal given on the decision notice to see whether these relate to matters of principle or to technical objections that might be overcome by a revised proposal.

You should discuss the reasons for refusal with the planning officer who dealt with the application to gauge the strength of the case that is likely to be mounted against the proposed development. You should seek an informal opinion from him or her on whether an amended scheme is likely to be acceptable. Most planning officers are used to looking at the arguments from both sides and will talk openly about relevant considerations, often acknowledging where a decision has been marginal and the issues finely balanced. Where the planning authority has had relevant experience of a similar appeal elsewhere within its area, this is likely to be brought to your attention.

Try to establish whether the planning authority would prefer an appeal by the exchange of written representations or would be more likely to seek a hearing or public inquiry, as these have a significant bearing on the cost and likely duration of the process (see below). In the event of a public inquiry, find out if this is likely to be handled by the council's own officers or, especially where members have overturned a recommendation for approval by officers, whether consultants would be appointed. Also, ask whether the planning authority is likely to instruct counsel or rely on its own in-house solicitor to act as advocate.

The strength of third party opposition should also be considered and, in particular, how those parties would be likely to respond to an appeal. Well-organised and motivated objectors can be formidable opponents!

Other important considerations

Also bear in mind the following:

"On average, one-third of all appeals are successful"

- On average, about one-third of all appeals are successful.
- There are strict time limits for lodging an appeal and for the subsequent process.
- An appeal can only be made by whoever was named originally as the applicant (although this may, of course, be via an agent).
- An appeal for non-determination may result in a longer delay in securing permission than might otherwise have been the case had the planning authority been allowed more time to consider the application. However, the Planning and Compulsory Purchase Act 2004 ('the 2004 Act') has introduced the concept of 'dual jurisdiction', giving planning authorities additional time in which to

determine an application subject to such an appeal. At the time of writing, this provision has yet to take effect.

- In most cases, the resubmission of a similar application within 12 months of a refusal will not require the payment of a new fee to the planning authority. While there is nothing to prevent an unsuccessful applicant from submitting a revised proposal and at the same time lodging an appeal against a recent refusal, under section 43 of the 2004 Act planning authorities are able to decline to determine a fresh application for permission in certain circumstances. These include any new application similar to one recently refused by the Secretary of State, and so-called 'overlapping applications', such as where an earlier similar application has not yet been decided by the Secretary of State and the planning authority has made a decision, or has failed to do so within the determination period, but the time allowed for making an appeal has not yet expired.

- Appeals can be lengthy, time-consuming and expensive, especially where hearings and public inquiries may be required. However, the new fast-track HAS should make appeals against such minor developments easier. In addition, following recent reforms, it is now possible with all planning and enforcement appeals, including those where the written procedure is adopted, to seek an award of costs against a planning authority on the grounds of its unreasonable behaviour, although this may be difficult to prove. But, be warned – a planning authority may also seek an award against an appellant where he or she has behaved unreasonably and caused unnecessary expense to be incurred. Otherwise, the general rule is that parties are expected to pay their own expenses for an appeal, and these will depend on its complexity. The Inspectorate is likely to introduce an appeal fee sometime soon, based on a sliding scale of charges.

- An appeal can be withdrawn at any stage, but this may result in costs being awarded against the appellant.

- Under section 79 of the Town and Country Planning Act 1990 ('the 1990 Act'), an inspector or the Secretary of State (or, in the case of Wales, the National Assembly) is able to allow or dismiss the appeal, or reverse or vary any part of the decision of the local planning authority (LPA), whether the appeal relates to that part of it or not, and may deal with the application afresh. In addition, an appeal against conditions can result in others which have not been appealed being altered, further conditions added, or the loss of the entire permission itself, although the opportunity to withdraw the appeal will be given, thereby enabling the appellant to keep their existing permission. However, this situation can be avoided by first applying to the planning authority under section 73 of the 1990 Act to carry out development without complying with a condition of a permission and then appealing against any refusal or variation that is unacceptable.

- Under section 79(6A) of the 1990 Act, the Secretary of State may also dismiss an appeal where an appellant has been responsible for causing undue delay in progressing an appeal.

The different types of procedure

There are three types of procedure for dealing with planning appeals:

- written representations (in England, about 80 per cent of appeals are dealt with by this method, and around 75 per cent in Wales)
- hearing (commonly referred to as an informal hearing)
- local inquiry (generally referred to as a public inquiry).

In England, the number of planning appeals has risen sharply, from around 14,000 in 1997/98 to over 22,000 in 2007/08, although due to the changed economic climate the Inspectorate expects that this will have reduced by around 15 per cent during 2009/10.

Just over one-third of all appeals relate to householder development, which are normally quite straightforward. So, in order to speed things up, since 6 April 2009 the Inspectorate has operated an expedited appeal service to deal exclusively with householder development, with a target of issuing decisions within eight weeks.

Appeals that the Inspectorate considers suitable for the new householder appeals service (HAS) automatically involve an exchange of written representations (see below). For the rest, the Inspectorate will determine the procedure that the appeal will follow, in accordance with ministerially approved criteria. These are set out in *Procedural Guidance: Planning Appeals and Called-in Planning Applications* (PINS 01/2009), published by the Inspectorate in April 2009. The method of appeal will depend on the particular circumstances of the case, with the decision on this being taken following consideration of the preferences of both the appellant and the LPA. The Inspectorate stresses, however, that the type of procedure adopted has no bearing on the outcome of the appeal, which will always depend on its planning merits. Nevertheless, it is worth considering the following points:

- The *written procedure* is generally preferred by the Inspectorate and is by far the most commonly used method. It is also the simplest, cheapest and quickest. It is best suited to relatively minor proposals and/or where:
  - the grounds of appeal and issues raised can be clearly understood from the appeal documents plus a site inspection, and/or
  - the Inspector should not need to test the evidence by questioning or to clarify any other matters, and/or
  - an Environmental Impact Assessment is either not required or is not in dispute.

  But it is not suitable for every appeal, particularly where issues of fact are challenged or where the proposals are controversial and have generated significant local interest.

- A *public inquiry* may be requested by either the appellant or the planning authority where:
  - the issues are complex and likely to need evidence to be given by expert witnesses, and/or
  - the principal parties are likely to need to be represented by an advocate, such as a lawyer or other professional expert because material facts and/ or matters of expert opinion are in dispute and formal cross-examination of witnesses is required, and/or
  - legal submissions may need to be made.

  A public inquiry is the most formal of the procedures and is similar to a court of law, although it is less adversarial. This procedure is normally only used to examine large, complicated or controversial proposals.

- A *hearing* is more informal than a public inquiry, and may be suitable where the criteria for written representations are not met because questions need to be asked. Examples of suitable cases are where: the claimed status of an appellant as a Gypsy needs to be clarified; the need for the proposal is at issue, such as for an agricultural worker's dwelling or a traveller site; or the personal circumstances of the appellant require scrutiny, such as with proposals for people with disabilities or other special needs. In addition, the hearing method may be the most appropriate procedure where:
  - there is no need for evidence to be tested by formal cross-examination
  - the issues are straightforward (and so do not require legal or other submissions to be made), and

- ○ the appellant's case and that of the LPA and interested persons is unlikely to take more than one day to be heard.

  Hearings are therefore considered suitable for cases with issues that require some explanation, but where there is little or no third party interest and complex legal, technical or policy issues are not involved.
- The Inspectorate currently aims to determine 50 per cent of appeals within its target periods of 16 weeks for written appeals (eight weeks for cases dealt with by the HAS), 30 weeks for hearings (22 weeks in Wales) and 30 weeks for inquiries. These targets are subject to annual revision. In practice, in England the average length of time taken to determine a written planning appeal (other than those using the new HAS) has been 18 weeks, while that for hearings has been around 29 weeks and inquiries nearly 34 weeks. In Wales, average performance has been higher, with around 15 weeks for written appeals and 20 weeks and 28 weeks for those decided following a hearing or inquiry, respectively.

Time limits

It is essential to ensure that a valid, completed appeal is lodged within the relevant time limit. For a householder appeal, this is 12 weeks from the notice of the decision or determination giving rise to an appeal. For all other planning appeals, the deadline is six months from:

- the date of the decision, or
- the expiry of the statutory period within which an LPA should have decided the application, which is eight weeks for minor cases, 13 weeks for major developments and 16 weeks for applications accompanied by an Environmental Statement, or whatever extended period has been agreed with the LPA, or
- the date when further details were requested in support of an outline application, or
- such longer period as the Secretary of State may, at any time, allow. (It should be noted that while the Secretary of State has discretion to allow late appeals, this is only exercised in exceptional circumstances.)

Once the appeal has been lodged there is a strict timetable that must be adhered to, otherwise representations or other supporting documentation will be not normally be considered.

Written appeals

Documentation – Householder Appeals Service

In essence 'householder development' is defined as development of an existing dwellinghouse (other than a flat), or development within its curtilage for any purpose incidental to the enjoyment of the dwellinghouse. However, it does not include any changes of use.

Under the new HAS, the Inspectorate will be provided with a copy of the LPA's planning application file in an electronic format. The authority must rely solely on its decision notice, together with any internal reports, such as delegated and committee reports, to defend the appeal. It will not be allowed to provide a formal appeal statement or to attend the site visit. Neither will any third parties that objected to or commented on the application be given a further opportunity to make their views known.

The appellant must send in their full statement of case with their appeal form. The inspector will visit the site alone, with the appellant present in some cases only to provide access to the site.

So, as well as the appeal form itself, the papers required to lodge an appeal via the HAS are:

- a copy of the original application that was sent to the LPA, with any supporting documents
- a copy of the LPA's decision notice.

Documentation – non-householder development written appeals

For all other appeals, the following supporting documentation is also required:

- all correspondence with the authority relating to the application
- any ownership/agricultural holdings certificate provided to the authority
- a site location plan edged or shaded in red with any other adjoining land owned by the appellant, if any, edged or shaded in blue
- any other additional plans, documents or drawings relating to the application but not previously seen by the LPA, such as those amending the application. (However, acceptance of these will be entirely at the inspector's discretion. The Inspectorate is increasingly reluctant to accept changes and new material

at the appeal stage, preferring instead for these to be made before the application is determined. You should therefore be careful about this.)
- a list of all plans, drawings and documents submitted with the original application or as part of the appeal
- if the appeal relates to an application for approval of certain matters in accordance with a condition on a planning permission, the application for that permission, the plans submitted with that application and the planning permission granted.

The most important part of the appeal form is the section that requires the 'grounds of appeal' to be set out. The grounds should be set out in full, and it may be necessary to do this in a separate document. It is not sufficient to merely contradict the reasons for refusal; each ground of appeal should be supported by a reasoned argument. If the Inspectorate considers that these are inadequate it may seek further details or refuse to accept the appeal as valid. Depending on your experience of such matters and the issues involved, it might be wise to seek specialist advice from a planning consultant, although this may not be necessary in simple cases. In any event, it is important to ensure that submissions are clear, concise and business-like. Avoid extravagant or emotional language, and make sure that sufficient evidence is put forward to substantiate your claims.

Where the appeal is against the failure of the LPA to determine the application, the appeal form should set out the reasons why permission should be granted. Of course, where the application is supported by a Design and Access Statement, and you have followed our advice on writing such statements, this should be quite easy.

Timetable and procedure for non-householder written appeals

Once the appeal has been validated, an acknowledgement letter is sent out giving the name of the case officer and an official starting date for the appeal (the date of the letter). The letter also sets out the timetable, which is essentially as follows:

- Within 7 days of the receipt of a valid appeal, the Inspectorate will decide that the written procedure is the most appropriate method to be followed.
- Within two weeks from the starting date, the planning authority must submit a copy of an appeal questionnaire and supporting documents, including relevant development plan policies, committee minutes, the planning officer's

report (if there is one), copies of correspondence received from third parties and a list of conditions it would wish to see imposed should permission be granted. A copy of these papers is sent to the appellant. The questionnaire will identify whether the planning authority intends to submit a further written statement or, as the Inspectorate now prefers, simply rely on the initial documentation. If it does submit a further statement, there will be an opportunity to comment on it.

- Within six weeks of the starting date, the appellant must submit two copies of any statement detailing the case in support of the grounds of appeal. However, this cannot be used as an opportunity to introduce new grounds of appeal. If the planning authority has indicated that it will be producing a similar statement of case, then two copies of this must also be submitted within this period. The Inspectorate will send each party a copy of the other's statement, together with copies of any correspondence received from interested persons in response to the requisite appeal notification procedures.
- Within nine weeks, both the planning authority and the appellant must submit to the Inspectorate two copies of any comments on the other's statement or on submissions by interested parties. However, no new evidence may be submitted at this stage. Any final comments are copied to the planning authority and appellant. By this stage, any planning obligation must be submitted by the appellant in its final form (that is, completed and signed).

These deadlines are strictly enforced by the Inspectorate and any late submissions will normally be returned. At the end of this period, the appeal file is sent to the inspector, who will consider the appeal. Usually, within about 12 to 14 weeks of the starting date, an inspector will carry out a site visit. If the site can be seen clearly from a public road and the parties have agreed, the inspector will do this unaccompanied. However, where it is necessary for the inspector to view the site from private land, they must be accompanied by the appellant (or their representative) and someone from the planning authority. If one party fails to arrive, the inspector will carry out the inspection alone or another visit will be arranged. Any interested person who has commented on the appeal and wishes to attend will normally be allowed to do so.

At the site visit, the inspector will introduce himself or herself, check who is present, outline briefly the procedure and make sure that the parties agree that the inspector is dealing with the correct set of plans. It will be stressed that the purpose of the visit is not to discuss the merits of the appeal or to listen to the arguments of any of the parties. Where someone fails to adhere to this advice, the inspector will be quick to intervene or will simply walk away from the person concerned. The inspector will ask the parties whether there are any physical features on the site or in the vicinity to which they wish to draw attention, or to confirm any features referred to in the submissions. Occasionally, an inspector may also look at the site from adjoining land (such as from an objector's property), but they will need to be accompanied by the main parties.

Figure 6.1 (page 125) summarises the main stages in a non-householder appeal following the written procedure.

Hearings

Hearings have become increasingly popular in recent years, and in England about 16 per cent of appeals are dealt with by this method (20 per cent in Wales). But although a hearing may be requested, it is up to the Inspectorate to decide whether this method would be appropriate, bearing in mind how complicated or controversial the case is.

Hearings are more relaxed and less daunting than public inquiries, and are quicker and cheaper. They involve a structured 'round table' discussion led by the inspector, based on previously submitted written statements (known as 'hearing statements'), which both the appellant and the LPA are required to submit. The hearing statement must set out the case that will be put forward at the hearing and include any maps or plans that will be referred to. In addition, it should include a list of any conditions or limitations to which the appellant would agree were the appeal to be allowed. The discussion may continue on the accompanied site visit. Legal representation is not normally allowed, and there is no formal cross-examination.

Before the close of the hearing, the inspector will ask whether any party wishes to make an application for costs, which may be awarded in the case of unreasonable behaviour (see *Costs*, page 127). If the appellant wishes to rely on a planning obligation, a draft should be submitted with the appeal or at the latest ten days before the date of the hearing and signed and completed by the time the hearing closes.

The timetable for hearings is essentially the same as for the written procedure, except that there is no longer a nine-week stage for final comments, which

FIGURE 6.1: *Stages in an appeal following the written procedure (non-householder)*

Timetable	Appellant	Local Planning Authority (LPA)	Third parties
Appeal lodged within the 6-month time limit	Submits form, grounds of appeal and all supporting documents to Planning Inspectorate and LPA		
Within 7 days of the receipt of a valid appeal, PINS will decide that the written procedure is the most appropriate method to be followed, taking into account ministerial criteria and views of the appellant and LPA			
Within 2 weeks from the starting date	Receives the LPA's questionnaire and any supporting documents	LPA sends out questionnaire and supporting documents and notifies interested persons of the appeal	Interested persons notified of appeal
Within 6 weeks from the starting date	Submits 2 copies of any further statement to Inspectorate. This should deal only with issues raised by the questionnaire and any supporting documents	LPA sends Inspectorate 2 copies of a further statement	Interested persons send Inspectorate any comments
Within 9 weeks from the starting date	Sends Inspectorate 2 copies of any final comments on the LPA's statement and on any comments made by interested persons. No new evidence is allowed at this stage	LPA sends Inspectorate 2 copies of final comments on appellant's statement and on any comments made by interested persons. No new evidence is allowed at this stage	
Inspector visits site (on average within 12–14 weeks of the starting date)			
Within 16–26 weeks the formal decision is issued			

Source: adapted from PINS guide *Making Your Planning Appeal*.

must now be made at the hearing itself. A hearing will normally be arranged within 10 to 20 weeks of the starting date of the appeal.

For England, the procedure for hearing cases is set out in the Town and Country Planning (Hearings Procedure) (England) Rules 2000, as amended in 2009. For Wales, relevant guidance is set out in *National Assembly Circular 07/2003: Planning (and Analogous) Appeals and Call-in Procedures,* which also includes the relevant regulations.

Local (or public) inquiries

Only about 5 per cent of appeals are dealt with by way of a local inquiry (more commonly known as a 'public inquiry') and, as an architect, it is unlikely that you will find yourself taking the lead in such an appeal. In most cases, a solicitor and/ or a planning consultant, probably acting together with counsel, will assume overall responsibility for managing the appeal. Nevertheless, from time to time, architects are required to take the stand at a public inquiry to explain or defend their proposals, and it is therefore helpful to understand a little about the process.

There are two different procedures, according to whether the appeal is to be decided by an inspector or by the Secretary of State. In many respects, the early stages of the process are similar to those for other appeals, although where an expert witness proposes to read out a statement at the inquiry (in other words, a 'proof of evidence') this must be submitted at least four weeks before the inquiry. If longer than 1500 words, it should include a summary; usually only the summary will be read out at the inquiry. Also, at least four weeks before the inquiry, a 'statement of common ground' must be submitted to the Inspectorate, detailing those points that have been discussed and agreed between the planning authority and the appellant.

At the inquiry, the planning authority will present its case first, with the advocate calling witnesses in turn. Each will present their evidence, either by reading out the 'summary proof', or by being led through their 'main proof' by the authority's advocate, examining the evidence briefly and perhaps reading out relevant extracts or answering specific questions. When this is complete, it is the turn of the appellant's advocate to cross-examine the planning authority's witness in an attempt to test the evidence and expose its weaknesses. When this has finished, there is an opportunity for the planning authority's advocate to re-examine the witness in order to clarify any matters that arose during cross-examination. This is essentially an exercise in damage limitation, with the planning authority's advocate attempting to win back or play down any significant concessions made by the witness. Next, the inspector may ask any questions of the witness.

When the planning authority has finished presenting its case, it is the turn of the appellant, following the same procedure. If there are interested persons present, for example objectors or representatives of amenity societies, they will normally be invited to have their say. The inspector may also allow them to question witnesses and be questioned themselves.

At some stage in the inquiry there will normally be a discussion on suggested conditions and the terms of any planning obligation that might be under consideration.

Normally, both the appellant and the planning authority will make a closing statement, summing up their respective arguments and highlighting any points won or lost during the course of the inquiry. The appellant has the final say.

As in the case of hearings, any application for costs should be made before the close of the inquiry.

Once the inquiry has closed, the inspector will carry out an accompanied site inspection but, unlike in the hearing procedure, is not able to listen to any further arguments about the merits of the proposed development. At this stage, the inspector will simply be looking at the physical features on or near the site, to which attention may be drawn by the parties if necessary.

The Inspectorate currently aims to decide 50 per cent of appeals by public inquiry within 30 weeks.

Costs

The parties to an appeal are normally expected to meet their own expenses. However, in all cases either the appellant or the LPA can apply for costs if they feel that the other party has behaved 'unreasonably'. In addition, interested persons (that is, third parties) can seek an award of costs where a hearing or public inquiry has been cancelled at a late stage because of some unreasonable behaviour on the part of the appellant or planning authority, thus involving unnecessary expenditure in preparing for the appeal. Only in exceptional circum-stances are third parties otherwise likely to be involved in making or facing a claim for costs.

Costs awards are not dependent on the outcome of the appeal. Simply because an appeal succeeds, it does not mean that the appellant is automatically entitled to recover expenses. Conversely, if the appeal fails the appellant is not normally liable for paying the LPA's costs. An application for costs will not influence the decision on the appeal, although there are some practitioners who consider that, in some circumstances, the overall planning case is strengthened by such a claim.

Applications for costs are dealt with separately from appeal decisions, and are usually considered at the end of the process. For an application to succeed, it must be made at the appropriate time, and one party must have behaved unreasonably and put the other party to an unnecessary expense.

On average, about 40 per cent of all applications for costs succeed. When con-sidering whether behaviour is unreasonable, the inspector will take account of whether an appellant is professionally represented. So, if you, as an architect, decide to pursue an appeal on behalf of a client, it is vital that you are aware of the risks involved, understand fully the implications of your actions and advise your client accordingly. If in doubt, you should consider employing a planning consultant.

Examples of unreasonable behaviour

The most common examples concern non-compliance with procedural require-ments or failure by the planning authority to substantiate a stated reason for refusal. Other examples include the following (the list is not exhaustive):

On the part of the LPA

- Ignoring relevant national policy, including where this has superseded the authority's own policy in its development plan.
- Acting contrary to, or not following, well-established case law.
- Persisting with objections to a scheme, or part of a scheme, that has already been granted permission or which the Secretary of State or an inspector has previously indicated to be acceptable.

- Not determining similar cases in a consistent manner – for example, imposing a spurious additional reason for refusal on a scheme that is similar to one previously considered by the planning authority and where circumstances have not materially changed.
- Failing to grant a further permission for a scheme that is the subject of an extant or recently expired permission and where there has been no material change in circumstances.
- Refusing to approve reserved matters when the objections relate to issues that should already have been considered at the outline stage.
- Imposing a condition that is not necessary, precise, enforceable, relevant to planning, relevant to the development permitted or reasonable and thereby does not comply with the advice in DoE Circular 11/95 on planning conditions.
- Requiring the appellant to enter into or complete a planning obligation that does not accord with the tests in DETR Circular 05/2005 on planning obligations.
- Not imposing conditions on a permission where these could effectively have overcome the objection identified – for example, in relation to highway matters.
- Unreasonably refusing to enter into pre-application negotiations, contrary to paragraph 12 of PPS1, or to provide reasonably requested information, when a more helpful approach would probably have resulted in the appeal being avoided altogether.

On the part of the appellant

- Where the proposal is clearly contrary to national planning policy or the development plan and no – or very limited – other material considerations are advanced, with inadequate supporting evidence to justify determining otherwise.
- The appeal follows a recent appeal decision in respect of the same, or very similar, development on the same, or substantially the same, site where the Secretary of State or inspector has decided that the proposal is unacceptable and circumstances have not changed materially in the intervening period.
- The appellant is seeking permission for development in the Green Belt, which would be inappropriate according to *PPG2: Green Belts*, but has not demonstrated what the very special circumstances are or provided evidence to justify an exception to general Green Belt policy.
- The appellant has refused to enter into or provide a planning obligation or fails to provide an obligation in appropriate terms, which the Secretary of State or inspector considers is clearly necessary to make the proposed development acceptable.

- Withdrawal of the appeal or grounds of appeal.
- Deliberately unco-operative behaviour.
- Failing to respond to reasonable, timely and clearly stated requests from the planning authority for information or evidence on a major issue at the application stage, including any information attached to the decision notice, and then doing so at the appeal stage.
- Introducing new grounds of appeal or issues late in the proceedings.

The decision on an application for costs is normally made at the same time as the appeal decision. Neither the Secretary of State nor inspectors determine the amount of any costs payable, which do not include any compensation for indirect losses suffered, for example as a result of the delay in obtaining permission. It is therefore up to the parties to the appeal to negotiate these. Where agreement cannot be reached on the amount of the award, the matter must be referred to a taxing officer of the Supreme Court for resolution.

In England, further information on appeal costs can be found in *CLG Circular 03/ 2009: Costs Awards in Appeals and other Planning Proceedings* and in *Costs Awards in Planning Appeals (England): A guide for appellants* (CLG, July 2009). For Wales, see *WO Circular 23/93: Award of Costs Incurred in Planning and Other (including Compulsory Purchase Order) Proceedings*.

The decision on the appeal

In general, appeal decisions are issued within about four to seven weeks of the inspector's site visit. Most follow the same format and will:

- summarise the appeal details and decision
- discuss briefly any procedural matters
- summarise relevant development plan policy
- identify the main issues and set out the reasons for the decision
- include a note setting out the circumstances in which the validity of the decision may be challenged by application to the High Court.

Challenges: statutory and judicial reviews

Statutory review

In effect, an appeal decision is final unless successfully challenged through the courts – this procedure is known as 'statutory review'. However, such a challenge cannot be mounted simply because someone is unhappy with the outcome. It is necessary to demonstrate, for example, that an inspector has failed to give adequate reasons for the decision or to consider a matter that ought to have been taken into account. Basic errors, such as failing to comply with relevant requirements or exceeding statutory powers, misinterpreting relevant legislation or policy guidance, or misunderstanding the application in some fundamental way are also grounds for a challenge. If the challenge is successful, the decision will be quashed and the case remitted to the Secretary of State for redetermination. But that does not necessarily mean that the original decision will be reversed (although in some cases it will), rather that in the new decision the defect will be corrected.

Statutory challenges may be made by 'a person aggrieved' by the decision, which can include not only the appellant but also, in the case of an appeal that has been allowed, third parties and the LPA.

Applications to the High Court for leave to challenge an appeal decision must be made within six weeks from the date of decision. Because of the complexity and financial consequences of embarking on such a course of action, legal advice should always be sought beforehand.

Judicial review

Although there are significant differences, there is a similar right to challenge the decision of an LPA 'on a point of law'. This is known as 'judicial review'. Because this procedure is rarely appropriate where the right of appeal exists against a planning refusal, a judicial review is normally only brought by a third party against a planning approval. As with the statutory review, leave to pursue the challenge must be granted by the courts and the applicant must establish sufficient *locus standii* (that is, the right to take action or be heard by a court). An application for a judicial review must be made promptly, and in any event within three months; anyone considering such action should therefore take legal advice as soon as it is known that an application is likely to be, or has been, approved.

Complaints to the council or Ombudsman

Both the Planning Inspectorate and LPA have procedures for dealing with complaints about the way in which an appeal or application has been handled.

In serious cases, where an applicant or appellant feels that they have been treated unfairly through maladministration or have had problems in obtaining access to official information, it might be necessary to consider making a complaint to the appropriate Ombudsman:

- *In the case of the Planning Inspectorate*, the Parliamentary Ombudsman (also called the Parliamentary Commissioner for Administration). The Parliamentary Ombudsman cannot be approached directly and will only deal with a matter once it has been referred by an MP. Although able to make various recommendations, the Parliamentary Ombudsman is not able to alter the inspector's decision in any way.
- *In the case of a local planning authority*, the Local Government Ombudsman (there are separate ombudsmen for England and Wales). Complaints must be about maladministration, but only where this has caused significant injustice to the complainant (this includes financial loss or other hardship). The Local Government Ombudsman will not consider a complaint if the injustice is not great enough to justify an investigation, or where the matter is the subject of a planning appeal or review by the courts.

Maladministration covers such things as:

- unreasonable delay
- failure to adhere to the authority's own rules or the law
- bias
- the use of improper considerations
- the giving of wrong information

but the actual merits of any decision will not be investigated. The procedures in England and Wales differ only slightly.

In England, before the Ombudsman can investigate a complaint, the council must first be given a reasonable opportunity to deal with the matter. This is normally done through a councillor. Complaints must be made within 12 months of the matter becoming known and in writing, with supporting documentation. The Ombudsman will notify the council of the complaint, and invite its comments, and where appropriate carry out an investigation and produce a report and recommendation. Councils are not obliged to accept the Ombudsman's recommendations, but in nearly every instance they will.

In successful cases, recommended remedies can include the council having to make payments to the complainant (for example, where some loss in property value has resulted), together with meeting the costs of pursuing the complaint. It should be noted, however, that as the Ombudsman does not consider that it is usually necessary to use a professional adviser's services in order to make a complaint, it is unlikely to ask the council to pay such fees, other than in exceptional circumstances.

For further information, visit www.lgo.org.uk (the Local Government Ombudsman for England), or www.ombudsman-wales.org.uk (the Public Services Ombudsman for Wales).

Human rights

Since the principles of the European Convention on Human Rights were enshrined within the Human Rights Act 1998, which came into force in October 2000, it is sometimes argued that the planning system has violated an individual's human rights in one way or another. Typically, these arise in extreme enforcement cases, or those involving Gypsies and travellers, and from claims that there has been a breach in:

- article 1 of the First Protocol, which deals with the peaceful enjoyment of one's possessions and protection of property
- article 8, which confers a qualified right to respect for private and family life and for the home.

However, on appeal to the Secretary of State or in the European Court, claims that there has been a violation of a person's human rights have rarely succeeded, and only where the interference in the right of the individual concerned is not outweighed by the wider public interest, such as the preservation of the environment.

SUMMARY

- A planning appeal should be an act of last resort and be considered only when all else has failed.
- Appeals are made to the Secretary of State, but will be handled by the Planning Inspectorate – transferred jurisdiction allows inspectors to make appeal decisions (although in some circumstances the Secretary of State may recover jurisdiction and decide the appeal).
- Applicants may appeal against a decision in full, certain parts of a decision (such as the application of conditions) or the lack of any decision.
- Before lodging an appeal, make sure you fully understand the reasons behind the decision – talk to the planning officer to gauge how strong the opposition is and assess whether it would be possible to overcome this through a revised proposal. Make sure you consider all the implications of going through the appeals process.
- An appeal may be dealt with by written representations, a hearing or a public inquiry – although only relatively few are considered at a public inquiry. A new fast-track service has been introduced to deal with householder appeals.
- The procedure for each type of appeal is decided by the Inspectorate and formally established – make sure you follow the procedure and the strict time limits laid down.
- If you pursue an appeal that clearly stands little chance of success, fail to adhere to procedural requirements or otherwise behave unreasonably, you may be liable for paying the local authority's costs!
- In addition to the planning appeals process, a decision may be challenged through statutory or judicial reviews, although these only apply in special circumstances, generally related to the conduct of an appeal rather than the merits of a planning decision. In some cases, the Ombudsman may be approached if you are dissatisfied with the performance of the planning authority or inspector.

Section 7
Before commencing development, changes and breaches of planning control

In this Section:

- *Before you start work on site: discharge the conditions!*
- *Other consents*
- *Changes and minor amendments*
- *Breaches of planning control*

Before you start work on site: discharge the conditions!

A permission will lapse unless development is started within the specified time limit. The courts have ruled that the commencement of development includes various operations, such as certain site clearance and ground works.

However, before development is commenced, it is essential to check that all relevant planning conditions have been discharged and complied with. Failure to comply with any condition that requires something to be done before building work starts (these are known as a 'condition precedent' or 'pre-condition') may result in a failure to keep the permission alive. This means that the entire development could be unauthorised and therefore exposed to the risk of enforcement action, with the potential for the complete loss of the permission if it were for a development allowed in circumstances that no longer apply or against a policy background that is no longer valid.

Following a clumsily worded recent change in legislation that is open to different interpretations, and the related guidance in CLG Circular 04/2008 on fees which is disputed by many, practice for discharging conditions or for seeking confirmation of their compliance varies from authority to authority. The majority of English authorities now insist (incorrectly in our opinion) that requests to discharge planning conditions must be made formally and accompanied by a fee. However, some authorities continue to discharge conditions informally following consideration of a letter outlining required details and enclosing any drawings. You should therefore discuss the procedure with the appropriate planning authority. But whatever procedure must be followed, it is essential that you get written confirmation of the discharge of conditions.

In response to recommendations in the Killian Pretty Review, the government is currently looking at ways to streamline the process for discharging conditions.

Other consents

Do bear in mind that a grant of planning permission does not, of course, override the need, where appropriate, for consent under other legislation. The most obvious example is Building Regulations approval. In some circumstances, conservation area or listed building consent will also be required, as well as licences under environmental health or wildlife protection acts.

Changes and minor amendments

It is quite common, once permission has been granted, for developments to change during construction: in response to the altered requirements of the client, the need to satisfy statutory codes (such as Building Regulations or fire regulations) or simply because of some consideration or oversight on the part of the builder. In other cases, development might proceed with no permission at all, either unwittingly because it is incorrectly assumed that permission is not required, or sometimes in a deliberate attempt to flout the system. However, while it is not a criminal offence to carry out development without first obtaining the necessary authorisations (other than in certain cases, including where listed building, conservation area or Tree Preservation Order (TPO) consent is required), generally this is not a good idea and may cause significant problems when valuing or trying to dispose of the land concerned.

In recent years, planning authorities have generally abandoned the practice of sanctioning minor amendments to a permission informally, by a letter written by a planning officer. Instead, they have normally insisted on the submission of a fresh application for permission that follows the statutory process and allows for full consultation with others. In an effort to make it easier to obtain ratification of minor amendments, the Planning Act 2008 gives planning authorities the express power to make 'non-material' changes to planning permissions. In England, it will soon be possible to make applications for these changes on a standard application form and the local planning authority (LPA) must issue a decision within 28 days. No Design and Access Statement is required for the new type of application.

Nevertheless, many believe this new procedure will be of no, or very limited, practical value. Consequently, the government has also been considering ways to allow developers to make minor *material* changes to a permitted scheme without having to incur the expense and delay of going through the formal planning application process all over again. In response to the conclusions of the *Minor Material Changes to Planning Permissions: Options study*, prepared by WYG Planning & Design and published by CLG in July 2009, the government has implemented certain measures to allow section 73 of the Town and Country Planning Act 1990 ('the 1990 Act') to be used more effectively as a route for authorising more significant changes. The intention is to make it easier for a section 73 application to vary any condition that lists approved drawings, so that it refers to substitute drawings that show the desired changes.

Since this is another area of planning control where current practice varies, until the new procedures are fully up and running you should speak to the relevant authority.

As explained earlier, section 73A of the 1990 Act specifically enables an application to be made retrospectively to regularise an unauthorised development, although this cannot be done in the case of listed building or conservation area consent.

Breaches of planning control

LPAs are equipped with various powers to remedy serious breaches in planning control:

- The power to serve a 'planning contravention notice' where it appears that there has been a breach of planning control and the planning authority requires further information about activities on the land and details of owner-ship/occupation. In effect, this is often a shot across the bows.

- The power to serve an 'enforcement notice' to require certain steps to be taken to remedy any breach of planning control or for specified activities to cease within a stated period for compliance.
- The power to serve a 'breach of condition notice' where there is failure to comply with any condition or limitation imposed on a grant of planning permission. The period for compliance is normally 28 days unless a longer period is agreed. Failure to comply is a finable offence.
- The ability to seek a court 'injunction' to restrain any actual or expected breach of planning control.
- The power to serve a 'stop notice', or a temporary stop notice for a period of 28 days, to prohibit the use of land, for example as the site for a caravan occupied as a person's only or main residence, and to make a stop notice immediately effective where special reasons justify it.

Powers are also available to enforce against breaches of the special controls relating to listed building, conservation area, TPO, hedgerow and advertisement regulations and other consents.

LPAs have a general discretion to take enforcement action when they consider it 'expedient' to remedy a breach of control that would cause serious harm to public amenity or some other interest of acknowledged importance. They should not therefore instigate formal enforcement proceedings against a minor breach of control that causes no harm to local amenity. In addition, any enforcement action should always be proportionate to the breach of planning control and follow efforts to persuade the owner or occupier of the site to volun-tarily remedy the harmful effects of unauthorised development, including where it might be made acceptable by the imposition of conditions, inviting the submis-sion of a planning application. Local authorities are encouraged to exercise parti-cular care when considering enforcement proceedings against small businesses, the self-employed and private householders.

There are potentially significant penalties for contravening the requirements of an effective enforcement notice or the prohibition in a stop notice. Following successful prosecution in the courts, a convicted person can be fined up to £20,000, and the extent of such a fine will take into account any financial benefit that has accrued, or appears likely to accrue, as a consequence of the offence.

Appealing against enforcement action

While there is a right of an appeal in the usual way against an enforcement notice, no similar appeal can be made to the Secretary of State (or National Assembly for Wales) against a breach of condition notice, stop notice or injunction. Where an appeal against an enforcement notice is contemplated, bear in mind:

- anyone with a legal interest in the land which is the subject of the notice is entitled to appeal (that is, owner, tenant, etc.)
- the completed appeal must be lodged before the notice takes effect (this is usually 28 days after it has been served)
- once the appeal has been lodged, the notice is suspended pending the outcome of the appeal
- it is possible to appeal on various legal and planning grounds, and thus it is advisable to seek the advice of a planning consultant or planning solicitor
- the appeal includes a deemed application for planning permission
- a fee is normally payable to both the Planning Inspectorate and the LPA
- in certain circumstances, costs may be awarded where one party to the appeal has behaved unreasonably.

There are time limits for taking enforcement action against breaches in planning control, after which the development becomes 'immune' from such proceedings. In short, these are:

- operational development (see Section 5, *Is permission necessary?* page 54 for a definition) – four years from the date that these were substantially completed
- change of use to a single dwellinghouse – four years from the date of the breach in control
- all other breaches of planning control, including other material changes in the use of land – ten years.

However, there are *no* time limits for issuing listed building or conservation area enforcement notices.

Further general information on enforcement may be found in *Planning Policy Guidance 18: Enforcing Planning Control*, issued in 1991, and more detailed advice in *DoE Circular 10/97: Enforcing Planning Control*. The Planning Inspectorate has also published Procedural Guidance: *Enforcement Appeals and Determination of Appeal Procedure* (PINS 02/2009).

SUMMARY

- Planning permission may lapse if development does not commence within the specified time.
- Before commencing work, ensure that all relevant planning conditions have been discharged properly in writing and complied with. Check also that you have all the other consents in place that may be required under non-planning legislation.
- If plans have changed in any way from those submitted for planning permission, make sure that your planning officer has been informed – a revised planning application may be required.
- Local planning authorities are empowered to remedy breaches in planning control – make sure you understand what actions may constitute a breach.
- You may have grounds to appeal against enforcement action – but get professional advice before you do!

SOME FINAL THOUGHTS

For any architectural practice, large or small, stepping into the planning maze can prove to be a daunting experience.

We hope that this guide will help, and we are sure that you will not fall into the biggest trap: that having read the guide through cover to cover you think you know it all! Beware, there will still be a few blind alleys ahead and unseen pits to fall into. It therefore makes good sense to cultivate a working relationship with a local planning consultant to whom you can go for additional help, advice and guidance. After all, you would not attempt brain surgery all by yourself using only a surgeon's 'do-it-yourself kit'. And by now, you will have realised that involvement in the planning process can be just as complicated and perilous, and perhaps for some of your clients who are faced with a planning refusal the effect could appear just as fatal.

In the preface, we warned of the need to monitor the continuing changes to the evolving planning system. Whether they are major or minor, the implications of these adjustments will be significant. So it is vital that you keep your eye on the ball and stay up to speed. As we have already pointed out, 'constant change is the steady state'. This is especially true in today's complex and evolving planning world.

Appendix A

Main sources of further information and assistance

National planning policies and guidance

Note: most of following may be downloaded from the website of the Department for Communities and Local Government (CLG) at www.communities.gov.uk (for English policies and guidance) and the National Assembly for Wales at www.wales.gov.uk (for Welsh policies and guidance).

For England

These are the current Planning Policy Statements (PPSs)

PPS1:   Delivering Sustainable Development (2005). See also companion guides: *Safer Places: The planning system and crime prevention* (2004), *The Planning System: General Principles* (2004) and *Planning and Climate Change – Supplement to PPS1* (2007).

PPS3:   Housing (2006). See also companion guides: *Delivering Affordable Housing* (2006) and *Manual for Streets* (2007).

PPS6:   Planning for Town Centres (March 2005).

PPS7:   Sustainable Development in Rural Areas (2004).

PPS9:   Biodiversity and Geological Conservation (August 2005). See also ODPM Circular 06/2005 and *Planning for Biodiversity and Geological Conservation: A Guide to Good Practice* published in March 2006.

PPS10:   Planning for Sustainable Waste Management (July 2005). See also companion guide to PPS10 *Planning for Sustainable Waste Management* (June 2006) and Defra *Waste Strategy for England 2007*.

PPS11:   Regional Spatial Strategies (2004) and Technical Amendments (January 2009).

PPS12:   Local Spatial Planning (2008). See also accompanying *Plan Making Manual* on PAS website.

PPS22:   Renewable Energy (2004). See also its companion guide *Planning for Renewable Energy* (December 2004).

PPS23:   Planning and Pollution Control (2004).

PPS25:   Development and Flood Risk (2006).

These are the current Planning Policy Guidance notes (PPGs)

PPG2:   Green Belts (January 1995).

PPG4:   Industrial, Commercial Development and Small Firms (November 1992). To be amalgamated with other PPSs. A consultation draft entitled *Planning for Prosperous Economies* was published in May 2009 and seeks to combine guidance in PPG4, PPG5, PPS6 and parts of PPS7 and PPS13.

PPG5:   Simplified Planning Zones (November 1992).

PPG8:   Telecommunications (August 2001).

PPG13:   Transport (2001).

PPG14:   Development on Unstable Land (April 1990), together with Annex 1, Landslides and Planning (March 1996) and Annex 2, Subsidence and Planning (2002).

PPG15:   Planning and the Historic Environment (September 1994). To be replaced by a new PPS, which will combine PPG15 with PPG16. See consultation paper published in July 2009, Circular 01/2007 and Circular 07/2009.

PPG16:   Archaeology and Planning (November 1990). To be replaced by a new PPS (see above).

PPG17:   Planning for Open Space, Sport and Recreation (July 2002). See also companion guide *Assessing Needs and Opportunities* (September 2001).

PPG18:   Enforcing Planning Control (December 1991). See also Good Practice Guide and Circular 10/97.

PPG19:   Outdoor Advertisement Control (March 1992). See also Circular 03/2007.

PPG20:   Coastal Planning (September 1992).

PPG24:   Planning and Noise (September 1994).

Note: PPG21: Tourism (November 1992) was replaced in September 2006 by *Good Practice Guidance on Planning for Tourism*.

For Wales

Planning Policy Wales (PPW) (March 2002) is accompanied by a guide issued in 2006 and has been updated by the following Ministerial Interim Planning Policy Statements (MIPPS):

MIPPS 01/2009 – Planning for Sustainable Buildings (07/05/09)
MIPPS 01/08 – Planning for good design (07/02/08)
MIPPS 01/2006 – Housing (23/06/06)
MIPPS 02/2005 – Planning for Retailing and Town Centres (01/12/05)
MIPPS 01/2005 – Planning for Renewable Energy (01/12/05)

In addition, the following Technical Advice Notes (Wales) (TANs) supplement PPW:

TAN1:   Joint Housing Land Availability Studies (2006)
TAN2:   Planning and Affordable Housing (2006)
TAN3:   Simplified Planning Zones (1996)
TAN4:   Retailing and Town Centres (1996)
TAN5:   Nature Conservation and Planning (2009)
TAN6:   Agricultural and Rural Development (2000)
TAN7:   Outdoor Advertisement Control (1996)
TAN8:   Renewable Energy (2005)
TAN9:   Enforcement of Planning Control (1997)
TAN10:   Tree Preservation Orders (1997)
TAN11:   Noise (1997)
TAN12:   Design (2009)
TAN13:   Tourism (1997)
TAN14:   Coastal Planning (1998)
TAN15:   Development and Flood Risk (2004)
TAN16:   Sport and Recreation (2009)
TAN18:   Transport (2007)
TAN19:   Telecommunications (2002)
TAN20:   The Welsh Language – Unitary Development Plans and Planning Control (June 2000)
TAN21:   Waste (November 2001)

Regional Spatial Strategy/Planning Guidance (England only)

RSS: The North East of England Plan: Regional Spatial Strategy to 2021

The London Plan, Spatial Development Strategy for Greater London 2004, altered in 2006
RSS: The East Midlands Regional Plan to 2026
RPG/RSS9: Regional Planning Guidance for the South East of England (2001)
RPG9A: Thames Gateway (2003)
RPG/RSS10: Regional Planning Guidance for the South West (2001)
RPG/RSS11: Regional Planning Guidance for the West Midlands to 2021 (2004)
RSS: The Yorkshire and Humber Plan (2008)
RSS: The North West of England Plan to 2021 (2008)
RSS: The East of England Plan to 2031
RPG3B/9B: Strategic Planning Guidance for the River Thames (1997)
Milton Keynes and South Midlands Sub-regional Strategy (2005)

Useful reference sources

Two indispensable works for anyone proposing to become heavily involved in planning matters are:

- *Encyclopaedia of Planning Law and Practice*: an exhaustive nine-volume loose-leaf reference work published by Sweet & Maxwell, which is also available on CD-ROM. Visit www.sweetandmaxwell.co.uk
- *Development Control Practice*: an invaluable five-volume guide, which includes best practice, legislation, policy statements, planning authority guidance and appeal decisions, with expert analysis of how these are applied in practice. It is published by Development Control Services Ltd (DCS) and is also available online and on a searchable CD-ROM. Go to www.planningresource.co.uk/appeals/DevelopmentControlServices

DCS also maintains a very large computer database of appeal decisions (over 150,000) known as COMPASS, which may be searched, for a fee, and selected copies bought. Go to www.compasssearch.co.uk

If you want a standard textbook to supplement the advice in this guide, try:

- *A Practical Approach to Planning Law* by Victor Moore (10th edn) Oxford University Press (2007); or
- *Telling & Duxbury's Planning Law and Procedure* by Robert Duxbury (14th edn) Oxford University Press (2009).

An inexpensive way to keep abreast of information on current and proposed planning legislation and guidance is to subscribe to *Planning Legislation*

Update, published both quarterly and monthly by e-mail by Peter Hakes, chartered town planner and environmental consultant, in association with Anglia Ruskin University. Go to www.planninglegislation.info

Planning is the weekly magazine for planning practitioners and is the official journal of the Royal Town Planning Institute (RTPI). Subscriptions are also available to non-members. In addition to having a comprehensive news section, it includes *Development Control Casebook*, a digest of interesting and significant planning appeals decisions, court challenges and Ombudsman cases. There is also a forum where readers' queries on practical points are answered. Many of the magazine's features, reports mentioned in its news stories and cases reported in the casebook section are available on www.PlanningResource.co.uk

Regeneration and Renewal is another magazine that includes relevant news stories and features. Go to www.regen.net

The RTPI Library and Information Service (LIS) has a collection of books and journals on a broad range of planning-related topics including practice and theory. The library has an online catalogue and operates an inquiry service. The LIS Manager can be contacted via e-mail at library@rtpi.org.uk or telephone 020 7929 9452.

The Campaign to Protect Rural England (CPRE) publishes a series of low-cost, easy-to-understand guides and leaflets and, while aimed at campaigners, these will be of interest to others engaged in the planning process. Its publication list may be viewed at www.cpre.org.uk

The Planning Portal is the government's online planning and Building Regulations resource for England and Wales, and provides a wide range of services. It explains how the planning system works and allows users to submit applications and appeals electronically, as well as providing access to the main planning legislation and other planning-related documents, reports and statistics. Visit www.planningportal.gov.uk

The Planning Advisory Service (PAS), which is funded by CLG, helps councils provide faster, fairer, more efficient and better quality planning services. This includes supporting them with developing and delivering their local development frameworks. It encourages continuous improvement through guidance tools, case studies, regional events and direct support. It is also a useful source of information for those working in the development industry. Visit www.pas.gov.uk

The PAS website also provides a link to the Advisory Team for Large Applications (ATLAS), which is part of the Homes and Communities Agency (previously known as English Partnerships). ATLAS's role is to help unblock the issues holding up large applications, increase the knowledge and expertise of councils in handling such projects, share good practice across the sector and act as a partner to councils and independent reviewer of large applications and issues. ATLAS is leading on developing and reviewing the use of Planning Performance Agreements (PPAs), which were formally introduced into the planning system in England in April 2008. A PPA is a project management tool that is used by both the LPA and the applicant to take forward a proposal through the planning process. However, PPAs are about improving the quality, not the speed, of the decision-making process, with collaboration being the key ingredient. See the PAS website for further details.

Planning Aid

Planning Aid is a free, voluntary service, offering independent professional advice and assistance on town planning matters. It is aimed at individuals, community groups and other voluntary groups who cannot afford to pay for commercial consultancy services. It can help people with their own planning applications or to comment on other people's applications. It is not a substitute for the services provided by local planning authorities, or for the services of a professional planning consultant. For information, contact the RTPI at www.rtpi.org.uk; in Wales, go to www.planningaidwales.org.uk

Useful websites

There is a plethora of useful websites dealing with planning-related matters. Here are just a few (these are grouped by subject area and not necessarily alphabetically):

- *Communities and Local Government (CLG):*
  www.communities.gov.uk/planningandbuilding/
  The planning directorate of CLG is responsible for the system of town and country planning in England, while the government offices for the regions are closely involved in the preparation of regional guidance, and ensure that local authorities' development plans and decisions on planning applications

are consistent with this guidance. The site includes details of current national planning policy and related planning information and guidance.

- *Welsh Assembly Government: www.wales.gov.uk*
  This site functions in much the same way as the CLG site and includes current Welsh planning policy and guidance, and related information.
- *Infrastructure Planning Commission: http://infrastructure.independent.gov.uk*
- *Royal Town Planning Institute: www.rtpi.org.uk*
  The RTPI is the professional institute for town planners. The site provides access to the Online Directory of Planning Consultants and the Library and Information Service, and has good links to other sites.
- *The Planning Inspectorate: www.planning-inspectorate.gov.uk*
  In addition to publishing a number of very helpful guides to the different appeals that can be lodged, this site has a useful selection of links to other sites. There are different sites for England and Wales.
- *Planning Magazine: www.planningresource.co.uk*
- *RIBAnet: www.ribanetconference.com*
  RIBAnet is an online community of RIBA members, who can register free at this site. A wide range of users, including sole practitioners, big-firm partners, students, specialist consultants and RIBA staff, share their knowledge in 15 separate topic areas, including planning. Members discuss individual planning issues and share their experiences of dealing with local planning authorities. For example: enforcement requiring the removal of PVC windows and their replacement with timber framed windows in a listed building.
- *Oultwood: www.oultwood.com*
  An index to local government sites, with links, which takes account of recent changes.
- *Arboricultural Association: www.trees.org.uk*
- *Building Research Establishment: www.bre.co.uk*
- *The Prince's Foundation: www.princes-foundation.org*
- *British Urban Regeneration Association: www.bura.org.uk*
- *Civic Trust: www.civictrust.org.uk*
- *Commission for Architecture and the Built Environment (CABE): www.cabe.org.uk*
  CABE is the government's adviser on architecture, urban design and public space and publishes a number of useful guides, including one on how to write, read and use design and access statements.
- *Department for Culture, Media and Sport: www.culture.gov.uk*
  See the section on heritage protection reform.

- *English Heritage: www.english-heritage.org.uk*
  An excellent range of services and publications is available here.
- *CADW (Welsh Historic Monuments): www.cadw.wales.gov.uk*
  The Welsh equivalent of English Heritage.
- *Department for Environment, Food and Rural Affairs: www.defra.gov.uk*
- *Department for Business, Enterprise & Regulatory Reform (BERR) (previously Department for Trade and Industry): www.berr.gov.uk*
- *English Historic Towns Forum: www.ehtf.org.uk*
- *Home Builders Federation (HBF): www.hbf.co.uk*
  HBF is the voice of the home building industry in England and Wales.
- *Natural England: www.naturalengland.org.uk*
  Responsible for conserving and enhancing the natural environment of England.
- *Countryside Council for Wales: www.ccw.gov.uk*
  The Welsh equivalent of Natural England.
- *Homes and Communities: www.homesandcommunities.co.uk*
  The national housing and regeneration agency for England (successor to English Partnerships).
- *Environment Agency: www.environment-agency.gov.uk*
  The government agency concerned mainly with rivers, flooding and pollution.
- *Government Offices for the Regions: www.gos.gov.uk*
- *Health and Safety Executive: www.hse.gov.uk*
- *Office of Public Sector Information: www.opsi.gov.uk*
  A good place to look for legislation, statutory instruments and other official publications.
- *British and Irish Legal Information Institute: www.bailii.org*
  A useful site for recent legislation and court cases.
- *Highways Agency: www.highways.gov.uk*
- *Information Commissioner's Office: www.ico.gov.uk*
- *The Institution of Civil Engineers: www.ice.org.uk*
- *Landscape Institute: www.landscapeinstitute.org*
- *Law Society: www.lawsociety.org.uk*
- *Local Government Association: www.lga.gov.uk*
- *Fit – Fields in Trust (formerly the National Playing Fields Association): www.npfa. co.uk*
  Aims to protect and improve playing fields. Publications include the *Six Acre Standard*, which sets out widely accepted minimum standards on open space and play provision.

- *Ordnance Survey: www.ordnancesurvey.co.uk*
  Main supplier of maps for planning applications, etc.
- *National Association of Local Councils (NALC): www.nalc.gov.uk*
  Represents the interests of town and parish councils in England.
- *The Planning Officers' Society: www.planningofficers.org.uk*
- *Royal Institute of British Architects: www.architecture.com*
- *Royal Institution of Chartered Surveyors: www.rics.org.uk*
- *Resource for Urban Design Information (RUDI): www.rudi.net*
  An independent web resource dedicated to urban design and placemaking.
- *Sustainable Development Commission: www.sd-commission.org.uk*
  The government's independent watchdog on sustainable development. See also www.defra.gov.uk/sustainable/government for further details of the government's approach.
- *Town and Country Planning Association: www.tcpa.org.uk*
- *The Local Government Ombudsman (England): www.lgo.org.uk*
- *The Public Services Ombudsman for Wales: www.ombudsman-wales.org.uk*
- *The Parliamentary and Health Service Ombudsman: www.ombudsman.org.uk*
- *Urban Design Alliance (UDAL): www.udal.org.uk*

Appendix B

The Town and Country Planning (General Permitted Development) Order 1995, as amended in October 2008 for England only: Schedule of Permitted Development

(Refer to Order for provisions)

1. Development within the curtilage of a dwellinghouse (Classes A–H)
2. Minor operations
3. Changes of use
4. Temporary buildings and uses
5. Caravan sites
6. Agricultural buildings and operation
7. Forestry buildings and operations
8. Industrial and warehouse development
9. Repairs to unadopted streets and private ways
10. Repairs to services
11. Development under local or private Acts or orders
12. Development by local authorities
13. Development by local highway authorities
14. Development by drainage bodies
15. Development by National Rivers Authority
16. Development by or on behalf of sewerage undertakers
17. Development by statutory undertakers
18. Aviation development
19. Development ancillary to mining operations
20. Coal mining development by the Coal Authority and licensed operators
21. Waste tipping at a mine
22. Mineral exploration
23. Removal of material from mineral-working deposits

24. Development by telecommunications code system operators
25. Other telecommunications development
26. Development by the Historic Buildings and Monuments Commission for England
27. Use by members of certain recreational organisations
28. Development at amusement parks
29. Driver information systems
30. Toll roads facilities
31. Demolition of buildings
32. Schools, colleges, universities and hospitals
33. Closed circuit television cameras

Note: for a simple visual guide to the new provisions on development within the curtilage of a dwellinghouse, go to www.planningportal.gov.uk/england/genpub/en/.

See also www.planningjungle.com for a comprehensive discourse on the recent changes in England, including links to other sites and relevant appeal decisions.

Appendix C

Town and Country Planning (Use Classes) Order 1987, as amended for England: Summary of Use Classes

Note: there are some differences in Wales.

Refer to Order and ODPM Circular 03/2005 for details and guidance on restrictions.

A1 Shops: including retail warehouses, hairdressers, undertakers, travel and ticket agencies, post offices, domestic hire shops, sandwich bars, internet cafes and some coffee shops, etc. where the sale, display or service is to visiting members of the public, but *excluding* amusement centres, laundrettes, motor fuel, motor vehicles and car hire, and the sale of hot food.

A2 Financial and professional services: including banks, building societies, estate and employment agencies, betting offices, professional and financial services, etc. where the services are provided principally to visiting members of the public, but excluding health and medical services.

A3 Restaurants and cafes: where the primary purpose is the sale and consumption of food and light refreshments on the premises.

A4 Drinking establishments: pubs and bars where the primary purpose is the sale and consumption of alcoholic drink on the premises.

A5 Hot food takeaways

B1 Business:
(a) offices not within A2
(b) research and development
(c) light industry

being a use that can be carried out in any residential area 'without detriment to the amenity of that area by reason of noise, vibration, smell, fumes, smoke, soot, ash, dust or grit'.

B2 General industrial: industrial processes not falling within class B1.

B8 Storage and distribution

C1 Hotels

C2 Residential institutions: including residential accommodation where a significant element of care is provided such as nursing homes and hospitals. Residential schools, colleges and training centres also fall within this class.

C3 Dwellinghouses: includes not more than six residents living together as a single household (including where care is provided) and communal housing for elderly or handicapped, unless a significant element of care is provided.

D1 Non-residential institutions: includes clinics, health centres, crèches, day nurseries/centres, non-residential schools, education and training centres, museums, public halls, libraries, art galleries, exhibition halls, places of worship and church halls.

D2 Assembly and leisure: includes cinemas, concert, bingo, dance and sports halls, swimming baths, skating rinks, gymnasia, other indoor or outdoor sports or recreations, excluding motorised vehicles or firearms.

Sui generis **uses:** These are uses that do not fall within any specified class and include:

- retail warehouse clubs
- theatres
- amusement centres and funfairs
- laundrettes
- the sale of motor fuel
- car showrooms
- car hire
- taxi businesses
- scrapyards
- hostels and houses in multiple occupation (HMOs)

- nightclubs
- casinos.

Note: the Use Classes Order (UCO) provides that a move between activities within the same class is not development and therefore does not require planning permission. The Town and Country Planning (General Permitted Development) Order 1995 (as amended) (GPDO) also specifies certain moves between the use classes as 'permitted development', thus not requiring express planning permission.

Appendix D

Policy documents you should check prior to submitting a planning application

- National planning policies and guidance in PPSs, PPGs and TANs (Wales only)
- Regional Spatial Strategies
- Saved policies from old-style Structure Plans, Unitary Development Plans and Local Plans
- New-style Development Plan Documents, such as the Core Strategy, Site Allocations and any Area Action Plan
- Supplementary Planning Documents

Note: at local level, the starting point should be the planning authority's Local Development Scheme.

Appendix E

Checklist of main planning considerations for a major development proposal

Note: this list is not exhaustive.

1. Site selection generally

Try to choose a site that accords with the development plan or otherwise performs well in sustainability and national planning policy terms.

- In many cases, a site will already have been identified in an adopted or emerging Local Plan/Development Plan Document/Unitary Development Plan.
- Check the provisions of the **development plan**, both site-specific and generally, any planning brief, design guide or other relevant Supplementary Planning Guidance/Document, and consider detailed planning requirements and highway standards.
- If there is no allocation, consider the need for a **sequential site search** in accordance with PPS6 and PPG13 (or PPW), having regard to:
  - location relative to existing service centres and those people likely to use the facility
  - accessibility to public transport, so as to reduce car-dependency
  - preference for reusing previously developed land/buildings
  - effect on overall travel patterns
  - issues of need, flexibility, suitability and availability.

2. Assess physical characteristics of preferred site and surroundings

- Consider both site **constraints** and **opportunities**:
  - context – nature and pattern of surrounding development, especially housing or incompatible ('bad neighbour') uses

- site size and shape
- boundary treatment (e.g. screening, presence of walls, fences, hedges)
- existing condition of site and buildings
- site coverage and 'scale of development' issues
- nature of existing uses
- opportunities to reuse existing buildings or remove unsightly ones
- presence of listed buildings, archaeological or other protected features
- ground conditions, changes in level, flood-risk and drainage issues
- known access/parking/traffic problems
- location and condition of trees, especially any that are protected by a TPO
- location in any conservation or other sensitive area
- 'abnormal constraints', including possible contamination, land ownership/ site assembly/acquisition issues and special designations
- scope for future expansion
- general opportunities for planning and community benefits.

3. Investigate the planning history of the preferred site

- Establish a **'fall-back position'** (that is, what you are lawfully able to do in planning terms, in any event – often important in traffic generation terms):
  - previous refusals/permissions (including effect of any unimplemented permissions) and appeal decisions
  - requirements of any previous planning obligation/condition
  - implications of any existing apparent breaches of control (e.g. failure to implement landscaping scheme or comply with pre-condition).

4. Consider how best to promote the development on the preferred site

According to time frame and circumstances, you need to consider whether to:

- promote development through the **emerging Local Development Framework process** (see Section 4 in this guide), prior to planning application (long route: assumes no existing allocation), or
- proceed straight to **planning application and, if necessary, appeal (but must be good grounds for expecting success).**

5. Consider your emerging development proposals

- Consider **effects** of emerging development proposals against:

- ○ **national and development plan policy**
- ○ **visual impact** (especially on setting of listed buildings or on character and appearance of conservation area) – scale, mass, height, design and external appearance of buildings, planting and other landscape treatment
- ○ **impact on neighbouring residential amenity**, especially as a result of activity levels, comings and goings, potential noise or lighting disturbance, storage/disposal of waste, etc.
- ○ **accessibility**, particularly to public transport, effects of **traffic generation** and need for highway improvements, pedestrian links, parking and cycling provision, layout generally
- ○ **other environmental impacts** (including those listed in Section 5 of this guide)
- ○ **employment generation/loss** issues
- ○ **retail impact**, if appropriate
- ○ need for any **enabling housing development** to support provision or to restore heritage asset
- ○ **special impacts**, e.g. on important natural or heritage assets.

6. Pre-application 'partnership' discussions and consultations

- • **Early discussion with LPA officers** necessary to establish:
  - ○ **preliminary views**/chances of success
  - ○ **type and form of main application**, e.g. outline, reserved matters, full permission
  - ○ **need for any special consents**, e.g. listed building consent and/or conservation area consent for demolitions
  - ○ **need for any impact assessments**, including formal Environmental Statement under relevant regulations, or 'informal' assessments, such as those dealing with:
    - – sequential approach to site selection
    - – transport considerations
    - – protection of heritage assets
    - – environmental issues, including decontamination (remediation), noise, ground stability and drainage conditions
    - – landscape/ecology/visual impact, as appropriate
  - ○ **key players** with whom to negotiate, both officers and members, and any outside the authority

- ○ **likely timetable** for dealing with applications
- ○ possible need for **planning obligations/contributions** or matters that might be dealt with by **condition**.
- **Consultation with interested parties**, including highway authority/agency, Environment Agency, other council departments (e.g. landscape, conservation).
- **Discussion with others**, such as local residents, town council, relevant community and amenity groups (e.g. Civic Trust), key members.

7. Assemble team of specialists, as necessary (preferably early in process)

- **Planning:**
  - ○ lead consultant and co-ordinator of specialist inputs
  - ○ preparation of design and access statement, and planning statement to, among other things:
    - – make 'overarching' case for granting permission, within policy context
    - – explain design principles and access considerations, and
    - – stress benefits and sustainability soundness.
- **Architect/designer:**
  - ○ overall design concept/response to project brief
  - ○ input to design and access/planning statement.
- **Transport consultants**, likely to deal with:
  - ○ transport assessment:
    - – defend location suitability in PPG13 terms
    - – accessibility to public transport/contributions to local bus service provision
    - – provision for pedestrians and cyclists
    - – green travel plan
    - – on-site and off-site highway improvements
    - – traffic generation.
- **Environmental consultants**, to address:
  - ○ ground conditions and decontamination measures
  - ○ landscape, natural assets and visual impact
  - ○ noise/light pollution assessment
  - ○ heritage assets impact assessment
  - ○ flooding and drainage.
- **Others**, which might include:
  - ○ legal (to advise on planning obligations)
  - ○ structural and other specialist engineers.

8. Submission of applications for permission/consent

- **Negotiations** with LPA officers and others:
  - ◦ If a proposal is in accordance with policy, there is rarely a need for 'planning gain', per se, but **planning obligation** or **developer contributions** may be required to address relevant issues.
  - ◦ If a proposal does not accord with policy, it must be possible to demonstrate 'other considerations' in its favour, such as **benefits** (or, in urban-edge Green Belt situations, 'very special circumstances').
- Consider **political dimension**, use of lobbying, member support and tactics generally.
- **Monitor progress** and anticipate potential outcome, including requirements for planning contributions and conditions.
- Consider need for **withdrawal** before refusal (to avoid negative history) followed by **re-submission**, or **deferral**, where possible (to provide additional information or negotiate amendments), or an **appeal** (as a last resort).

Key points for success

- Try to work within the framework of the development plan and government planning policy.
- Try to choose a previously developed site with good links to public transport and close to existing main facilities and services.
- Identify relevant issues and impacts early on and be prepared to use appropriate specialists to provide relevant impact assessments.
- Enter into early discussions with the LPA, consult interested parties, stakeholders, community representatives, and engage local residents and potential objectors.
- Stress the need for and planning/community benefits of the development and its sustainability credentials.

Documents referred to in this guide

Not including *PPS*, *PPG* and *TAN* publications (see Appendix A).

Barker, Kate (2004). *Barker Review of Housing Supply*. HM Treasury.

Barker, Kate (2006). *Barker Review of Land Use Planning*. HM Treasury.

BSI (2005). *BS 5837:2005 Trees in Relation to Construction. Recommendations.*

BSI (2007). *BS 6297:2007 Code of practice for the design and installation of drainage fields for use in wastewater treatment.*

Building Research Establishment (1991). *Site Layout Planning for Daylight and Sunlight: A guide to good practice.* BRE Report 209.

Commission for Architecture and the Built Environment (CABE) (2003). *Design and Access Statements – How to write, read and use them.*

Countryside Commission and Department for the Environment (1997). *Lighting in the Countryside: Towards good practice.* Available from CLG website.

Department for Communities and Local Government (CLG) (2006). *Planning Obligations: Practice guidance.*

CLG (2007). *Strategic Housing Land Availability Assessments: Practice guidance.*

CLG (2007). *Outdoor Advertisements and Signs – A Guide for Advertisers.*

CLG (2007). *The Validation of Planning Applications: Guidance for local planning authorities.*

CLG (2008). *Protected Trees – A guide to tree preservation procedures.*

CLG (2009). *Costs Awards in Planning Appeals (England): A guide for appellants.*

Department for Culture, Media and Sports and Welsh Assembly Government (2007). *Heritage Protection for the 21st Century.* Cm 7057.

Department for the Environment, Food and Rural Affairs (Defra). *The Hedgerows Regulations 1997: A guide to the law and good practice.*

Defra. *The Hedgerows Regulations: Your Question Answered* (leaflet).

Defra (2005). *One Future – Different Paths: The UK's shared framework for sustainable development.*

Department of Trade and Industry (2004). *Site Waste Management Plans: Guidance for construction contractors and clients.*

Department for Transport (DfT) (2007). *Guidance on Transport Assessment.*

DfT (2009). *Good Practice Guidelines: Delivering travel plans through the planning process.*

Department for Transport, Local Government and the Regions (2001). *Planning: Delivering a fundamental change* (Planning Green Paper).

Eddington, Sir Rod (2006). *The Eddington Transport Study.* HM Treasury.

European Parliament (2001). *European Directive 2001/42/EC of the European Parliament and of the Council on the Assessment of the Effects of Certain Plans and Programmes on the Environment.*

Greater London Authority (2004). *The London Plan.*

HM Government (2005). *Securing the Future: The UK Government Sustainable Development Strategy.* Cm 6467. Defra.

Killian, Joanna and Pretty, David (2008). *The Killian Pretty Review: Planning applications – A faster and more responsive system.* CLG.

Luder, Owen (2006). *Keeping Out of Trouble.* Good Practice Guide. RIBA Publishing.

National Assembly for Wales (2002). *Planning Policy Wales.*

National Assembly for Wales (2002). *Planning: Delivering for Wales.* Consultation paper.

National Assembly for Wales (2004). *People, Places, Futures – The Wales Spatial Plan.*

ODPM (1999). *Preparing Community Strategies: Government guidance to local authorities.*

ODPM (2000). *Tree Preservation Orders: A guide to the law and good practice.*

ODPM (2002). *Building Regulations 2000 Approved Document H – Drainage and waste disposal.*

ODPM (2002). *Code of Best Practice on Mobile Network Development.*

ODPM (2004). *Community Involvement in Planning.*

ODPM (2004). *Creating Local Development Frameworks: A companion guide to PPS12.*

ODPM (2004). *The Planning System: General principles.*

ODPM (2004). *Safer Places: The planning system and crime prevention.*

ODPM (2005). *Sustainability Appraisal of Regional Spatial Strategies and Local Development Documents: Guidance for regional planning bodies and local planning authorities.*

ODPM (2005). *Best Practice Guidance on the Validation of Planning Applications.*

ODPM. *Outdoor Advertisements and Signs – A guide for advertisers* (booklet).

ODPM, Defra and English Nature (2006). *Planning for Biodiversity and Geological Conservation: A guide to good practice*. ODPM.

Planning Advisory Service (2007). *Constructive Talk: Investing in pre-application discussions*. PAS.

Planning Inspectorate (2005). *Development Plans Examination – A guide to the process of assessing the soundness of development plan documents*.

Planning Inspectorate (2009). *Procedural Guidance: Planning Appeals and Called-in Planning Applications* (PINS 01/2009).

Planning Inspectorate (2009). *Procedural Guidance: Enforcement Appeals and Determination of Appeal Procedure* (PINS 02/2009).

Royal Town Planning Institute (2007). *New Vision for Planning*. RTPI.

Town and Country Planning Association (1986). *Citizen's Guide to Town and Country Planning*.

UCL and Deloitte (2007). *Shaping and Delivering Tomorrow's Places: Effective practice in spatial planning*. RTPI.

Welsh Assembly Government (WAG) (2006). *Local Development Plan Manual*.

WAG (2008). *People, Places, Futures – The Wales Spatial Plan: 2008 Update*.

WAG (2006). *Planning Your Community: A guide to Local Development Plans*.

WAG (2008). *Local Vision: Statutory Guidance from the Welsh Assembly Government on developing and delivering community strategies*.

WYG Planning & Design (2009). *Minor Material Changes to Planning Permissions: Options study*. CLG.

Government circulars

CLG Circular 03/2009: Costs Awards in Appeals and other Planning Proceedings.

CLG Circular 02/2009: The Town and Country Planning (Consultation) (England) Direction 2009.

CLG Circular 02/2008: Standard Application Form and Validation.

CLG Circular 04/2008: Planning-related Fees.

CLG Circular 03/2007: Town and Country Planning (Control of Advertisements) (England) Regulations 2007.

CLG Circular 01/2007: Revisions to Principles of Selection for Listed Buildings.

CLG Circular 01/2006: Guidance on Changes to the Development Control System.

ODPM Circular 09/2005: Arrangements For Handling Heritage Applications – Notification to National Amenity Societies Direction 2005.

ODPM Circular 08/2005: Guidance on Changes to the Development Control System.

ODPM Circular 06/2005: Biodiversity and Geological Conservation – Statutory Obligations and Their Impact Within the Planning System.

ODPM Circular 05/2005: Planning Obligations.

ODPM Circular 03/2005: Changes of Use of Buildings and Land.

National Assembly Circular 07/2003 Planning (and Analogous) Appeals and Call-in Procedures.

ODPM Circular 01/2001: Arrangements for Handling Heritage Applications – Notification and directions by the Secretary of State.

DETR Circular 03/99: Planning Requirement in respect of the Use of Non-Mains Sewerage incorporating Septic Tanks in New Development.

DETR Circular 6/98: Planning and Affordable Housing.

WO Circular 13/97: Planning Obligations.

DoE Circular 10/97: Enforcing Planning Control: Legislative Provisions and Procedural Requirements.

WO Circular 61/96: Planning and the Historic Environment: Historic Buildings and Conservation Areas.

WO Circular 60/96: Planning and the Historic Environment: Archaeology.

WO Circular 23/93: Award of Costs Incurred in Planning and Other (including Compulsory Purchase Order) Proceedings.

DoE Circular 11/95: The Use of Conditions in Planning Permissions.

DoE Circular 9/95: General Development Order Consolidation.

DoE Circular 15/92: Publicity for Planning Applications.

Index

Note: page numbers in italics refer to figures.